Mental Health and the Criminal Justice System

A Social Work Perspective

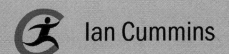 Ian Cummins

CRITICAL
APPROACHES
TO SOCIAL
WORK

First published in 2016 by Critical Publishing Ltd

British Library Cataloguing in Publication Data
A CIP record for this book is available from the British Library

ISBN: 978-1-910391-90-7

This book is also available in the following e-book formats:

MOBI ISBN: 978-1-910391-91-4
EPUB ISBN: 978-1-910391-92-1
Adobe e-book ISBN: 978-1-910391-93-8

Cover and text design by Greensplash Limited
Project Management by Out of House Publishing
Printed and bound in Great Britain by 4edge, Essex

Critical Publishing
152 Chester Road
Northwich
CW8 4AL
www.criticalpublishing.com

Paper from responsible sources

Dedication

For my wife Marilyn, and my sons Nelson and Elliot

Help us to help you!

Our aim is to help you to become the best professional you can be. In order to improve your critical thinking skills we are pleased to offer you a **free booklet** on the subject. Just go to our website www.criticalpublishing.com and click the link on the home page. We have more free resources on our website which you may also find useful.

If you'd like to write a review of this book on Amazon, Books Etc, or Wordery, **we would be happy to send you the digital version of the book for free**.

Email a link to your review to us at admin@criticalpublishing.com, and we'll reply with a PDF of the book, which you can read on your phone, tablet or Kindle.

You can also connect with us on:

Twitter   @CriticalPub#criticalpublishing

Facebook   www.facebook.com/Critical-Publishing-456875584333404

Our blog   https://thecriticalblog.wordpress.com

Contents

Lists of Tables and Figures

Tables

Figures

Meet the Author

Ian Cummins is senior lecturer in social work at the University of Salford. His main research revolves around the experiences of people with mental health problems in the Criminal Justice System with a focus on policing and mental illness. This is linked to an exploration of the development of the penal state and its interaction with community-based mental health services. He is interested in the ways the CJS has become, in many instances, the default provider of mental health care.

Acknowledgements

This work is based on my social work practice experience, academic research and teaching. I would like to thank my fellow social workers, academic colleagues and students for the opportunity to discuss and develop my ideas with them. The enthusiastic support of Donna Peach, Jameel Hadi, Sarah Pollock, Jo Milner and Kate Parkinson enabled me to finish this project. Scott Grant (Glasgow Caledonian University) and Karen Kinghorn (Salford University) very kindly read drafts of the book. Di Page at Critical Publishing has provided excellent support and advice.

Clarence the Angel says 'no man is a failure who has friends', so thanks to mine: Deryck Browne, Janet Chapman, David Edmondson and Christine Hayes; Marian Foley, Martin and Penny King; Gavin and Trisha Kendall; Jane Lucas, Bernard Melling, Bryn and Viv Morris; Lisa Morriss, Dave, Nick, Steve and Stuart Norwood; and Emma Palmer, Barry Schilling and Jonathan Simon for their friendship, support and coffee. Without them, I would not have completed this work.

Finally, I would like to thank my sisters, Helen, Denise, Kate and Colette and my brother, Michael, for all their love and support. This work is dedicated to them and my late mother Violet, who loved books.

Foreword

Many opinion leaders in both the UK and the US claim to be 'shocked' to discover the ubiquitous presence of people with serious mental (and often physical) illnesses in the jails and prisons of both countries. This shock may be genuine and the moral outrage it often gives rise to useful for those of us seeking deep reforms in our criminal justice systems, but it also belies the chain of public policy decisions taken in both countries over the last half century that has produced this result. The punitive turn in criminal justice policies was part of a larger shift in the governance of poverty (Wacquant, 2009) from the integrationist strategies of social democratic welfarism, to the exclusion and risk-management strategies associated with the neo-liberal 'consensus' of the past quarter century (Garland, 2001). The result in almost every society that has made this turn is a dramatic expansion of the prison population but was also preceded by a parallel abandonment of a social commitment to addressing the mental health needs of the poor. This neo-liberal governance of the poor, long presented as a project of being tough on both criminals and welfare recipients, is today emerging in the new light of a burgeoning crisis of chronic illness, both physical and mental. The valorization of personal responsibility as a foundation for citizenship finds its perfect expression in the structural violence of people shot to death by the police, suicided by jails without diagnosis or treatment, and prosecuted by courts legally blinded to the exigencies of mental illness.

We should be too nostalgic for the mental health policies that went along with the emerging welfarist policies of the post-World War II era. The large and coercive public hospital system built up in the nineteenth century became even more aggressive in its efforts to contain deviance in the post-World War II period and epitomized many of the flaws of social policy under welfare capitalism. Driven by the disciplinary ambitions and productivist fantasies of full employment of industrial societies that had experienced total war, mental health policy aggressively incorporated deviant behaviors and people of all sorts, whether a threat to anyone or not, into coercive systems of normalization. Involuntary commitment standards allowed people to be coercively confined on the basis of complaints by their families and neighbors or local police with little scrutiny as to what danger they posed to themselves or others, and (outside of expensive private hospitals) with little real effort at treatment.

Well before the punitive turn in criminal justice began, this coercive system of public mental hospital came under attack from sociologists, journalists, and mental health treatment survivors. Combined with advances in pharmaceutical treatments, and the shift in the mental health profession toward servicing middle-class patients with behavioral problems rather than profound psychoses, these criticisms soon found expression in new state policies in the US (and somewhat later in the UK) promoting the de-institutionalization of people with mental illness and a shift toward community-based treatment. The latter never developed: the first victim of the new political economic structural arrangements that would mark neo-liberalism.

The concern for patient dignity that had fueled the de-institutionalization movement faltered when it encountered new economic imperatives, especially the permanent fiscal crisis of the state and the increasing salience of high-end consumption activities to the urban economy and the related forms of mass private-property development. The promise of community treatment soon disappeared into a policy of wholesale abandonment. The gap was increasingly filled with incarceration. People defined as predators and threats to public safety had no call on individualized treatment at public expense.

While much has already been written about the punitive turn and neo-liberal social policy, this book is the first to place mental health and its relationship to criminal justice practices at the very center of analysis. The result manages to overview the empirical realities in the UK (and to some extent in the USA as well) of the failures throughout the criminal justice system to address mental health needs and use this crucial intersection to effectively introduce key concepts necessary to analyzing criminal justice and other institutions at the present conjuncture (including the incredibly important concept, via Antonio Gramsci and Stuart Hall, of the 'conjuncture').

Perhaps most importantly, this book is a concise call to action for how much can be done at this moment. The carceral state in both the US and the UK is at the very least experiencing a moment of instability and doubt, undergoing both retrenchment and redefinition (not unlike what welfarist institutions in the 1970s and 1980s experienced). This is not the moment to withhold our criticisms, because we know the results will not represent as radical a break with the current emphasis on punishment and exclusion, but it is equally important to point to sources of hope, transformation, and opportunities to restore balance and respect for human dignity.

Precisely because it is the darkest corner, the plight of people with mental illness in the arms of the criminal justice system is the most promising place to imagine reform, and the practice of probation is perhaps the most critical front. It once seemed as if mass incarceration had effectively swallowed the problem of deepening poverty in our increasingly unequal societies. With the poor defined as criminals, and mistreatment valorized as justice, neo-liberal social policy seemed beyond the capacity of science or rhetoric to expose. Today the humanitarian crisis in our prisons and in the policing on our streets is exposing itself to a public increasingly alarmed by the inhumanity and lack of dignity in these practices. As prisons and jails come under attack as both inhumane and inefficient, probation and other forms of community supervision are emerging as a preferred solution. At its worst, this shift may just mark a further stage of abandonment. At its best, this can the first stage of dissolving the carceral state and restoring the individuals and communities damaged by it.

There is no greater way for those engaged in the work of criminal justice to reaffirm the human dignity of all people in that system than to seek to understand and meet their health needs. The more frontline criminal justice practitioners are enabled to recognize and address those needs, the more often they will discover non-criminal justice answers the problems presenting as crimes, and create a positive legitimacy to the legal order that has a proven ability to reduce crime and violence. This is not to say that reform can achieve a fully dignified criminal justice system without addressing the larger structural sources of inequality in our societies. That would be to fall into precisely the kind of incomplete depiction of the problem that befell the de-institutionalization movement a biblical generation ago. It is to argue that the right analysis of criminal justice practice is for the present conjuncture absolutely critical to finding the limits of reform and the agenda of political change.

Jonathan Simon
Adrian A. Kragen Professor of Law, UC Berkeley, jssimon@berkeley.edu

Introduction

Critical questions

- *What role should social workers play in the CJS?*
- *What has been the impact of neo-liberal policies on the CJS and wider approaches to welfare?*
- *What are the major explanations provided for the increased use of imprisonment in the UK?*

The overall aim of this book is to examine the various ways in which the Criminal Justice System (CJS) interacts with mental health services. The CJS, at all stages, has now become a provider of mental health care and, in this chapter, I will outline the social work practice and research that underpins this work.

Background to my research

This book is based on my experiences as a probation officer, mental health social worker and academic researcher, with the starting point for this analysis being my work as a probation officer and social worker. I trained as a probation officer at a time when the probation service was very different from its current configuration, for its role has shifted dramatically in the past 15 years. The role of probation officer was set up by the Probation Act (1907), which formalised what had previously been the work of voluntary organisations, such as the Police Court Missionaries, who were funded by church-based temperance societies. The role of the probation officer was defined by the act to 'advise, assist and befriend' the offender. Modern probation officers are trained and qualified as social workers to work in the CJS. In addition to the expansion of the use of imprisonment, the past 20 years have seen the increased privatisation of sections of the CJS. Firms such as G4S have made significant profits from taking on roles that were previously seen as proper functions of the State. These have included running prisons and tagging offenders.

Before moving to an academic post, I worked as a mental health social worker and then approved social worker in inner-city Manchester in the mid-1990s. My interest in the broad themes of my research – policing and mental health, poverty, race and mental health, the failure of community care policies and the consequent impact on the CJS – can be traced back to that period. The team in which I was based covered one of the most deprived areas of the UK – at that time, the Local Health Authority was in the second poorest area of the country. This was a dynamic and challenging but, ultimately, very rewarding place to work as a social worker. When I read Kelly's (2005) work on the interplay between racism, poverty, gender, the CJS and mental health, I was very struck by his application of the term 'structural violence'. He uses the term as a tool for analysing the way that factors, such as race and mental health status, intersect to marginalise individuals and groups. This term, alongside Pierre Bourdieu's 'social capital', has become key for the development of my analysis. These concepts open up an approach that moves beyond the essentially sterile medical versus social models debates, which have dominated arguments in the mental health field. A new approach is required which acknowledges that mental distress has many social and biological causes. New solutions are required that address a range of factors, while ensuring that service users have a key input into the organisation and delivery of services.

Researching the CJS – working with the police

As a rather naive researcher, I approached Greater Manchester Police (GMP) with an idea to explore interviews carried out with an appropriate adult present. I was fortunate, as my request came at a time when general health issues in custody were being driven up the policy agenda. The Association of Chief Police Officers (ACPO) had just published its policy guidance for ensuring the safety and safer handling of detained persons (2006). A meeting was arranged with a senior officer at GMP with responsibility for custody issues. This meeting, on reflection, turned out to be one of the key moments of my research career. In focusing on the role of the appropriate adult, I had overlooked the wider processes in custody; GMP offered me the chance to look at wider mental health issues in custody. This shift involved approaching the issue from the perspective of those involved in the management of custody settings. The access being offered was priceless, so it would have been foolish not to have accepted this offer.

In my research, I have been very conscious of the importance of maintaining my professional identity as a social worker. This seems an obvious statement – I am clearly not a police officer. I had an understanding of the culture of custody and the importance of this rapport cannot be overestimated and, like Beynon (1983), I skilfully employed my professional background. The same was true in interviewing the officers in the initial study and in subsequent discussions about access to custody records. There are echoes here of Garfinkel (1967), who saw members of specialised groups as 'cultural colleagues' – the group here being professionals who work in custody settings. Garfinkel argues that an individual is a member of a group on the basis of the way that they are treated by others; in my case, this would include the use of 'institutional talk' – that is, the use of a specialised vocabulary or technical language. The custody environment and police discussion of it is replete with such terms – for example, *section 136* (police powers under the Mental Health Act, MHA), *PACE clock* (the time rules governing the length of time someone can be held in custody),

DP (detained person) and *FME* (Forensic Mental Examiner – a doctor called to assess an individual in custody). It was clear that officers acknowledged that my experience as a mental health worker in Manchester had given me an insight into these issues. I was aware of the importance given to 'real-life experience' in police culture; for instance, I would use case examples from my own work as a means of introducing topics. As Taylor and White (2000) argue, professional conversations reveal tacit understandings and knowledge. My understanding of this institutional talk was a key factor in establishing credibility with the police on both organisational and individual levels.

As I was working on the above empirical research, I additionally explored two interrelated areas: the socio-legal context and the development of community care. While I was involved in this work, the issues of policing and mental illness moved up the policy agenda. Over the course of this work, two major reviews were published, by Lord Bradley (2009) and Lord Adebowale (2013). The Bradley Review is a broader examination of the experiences of people with mental illness or learning disabilities in the CJS. Lord Adebowale's Inquiry was established following the death of Sean Riggs in order to examine deaths in custody. People with mental health problems are over-represented in these tragedies and Lord Adebowale extended his Review to look at the broader issues of policing and mental illness. I have examined these issues but seek to place them in the context of neo-liberalism and its impact on public services. I am strongly influenced by Foucault's notion of a 'history of the present'. What is important today has its roots in the past, but also in producing this history it creates a critical space to examine important areas; in this case, the impact of the failure of community care and the policy response.

As noted above, I was able to gain privileged access as a researcher to interview police officers and to review anonymised custody records. The custody setting is not a public space so the access that I was able to gain to interview custody sergeants placed me in an advantageous position as a researcher. The benefits are clear, in that I had access to information to, for example, parts of custody records that it would be very difficult to obtain under any other circumstances. In comparison, Reiner (2000a) uses the term 'outside outsider' to describe a researcher who is seen to lack the occupational and cultural capital by participants.

Appreciative inquiry as an approach

The starting point for research, in the social sciences, is that knowledge of the social world can be used to change it. This is in contrast to the natural sciences, where knowledge can produce understanding or new techniques but does not change the natural world. In my approach to exploring the role of the custody sergeant in the assessment and management of mentally distressed individuals in police custody, I have been influenced by appreciative inquiry (AI). Gergen (1994) argues that research should begin with appreciation. Social systems function in some way and are generally not in a state of complete entropy. In addition, research has to be applicable for it to have value. AI is based on a social constructivist, conceptual and ontological framework (Bushe, 1995; Chin, 1998; Cooperrider and Srivastva, 1987; Curran, 1991; Ludema, 2002). In this schema, language, knowledge and action are intertwined. An organisation or an aspect of it has to be viewed not only as the outcome of the actions of its members, but also in their interactions with the cultural, social and economic factors which shape that setting. As Michael (2005) notes, AI researchers argue that an appreciative approach produces a more nuanced understanding than one that starts from a negative proposition. AI has been used in CJS research – for example, Liebling et al's 1999 study of relationships in a prison and, more recently, Robinson et al's 2013 analysis of probation. In both cases, AI seeks to bring to the surface hidden areas of organisational culture.

AI sees research as generative: it attempts to produce change. AI notes that one of the most effective ways of doing this is to obtain the views of the marginalised within an organisation or system. Despite their key role, I argue that the little specific research into their work means that custody sergeants constitute such a group. It might seem odd to think of such powerful individuals as a marginalised group; however, it is important to look at their role within the organisation. Grant and Humphries (2006) describe AI as an approach that focuses on the positive attributes of organisational structures, which it sees as the basis for change. Rogers and Fraser (2003) suggest that there is an inherent danger that, by focusing on positive factors, AI risks distortion. AI can be contrasted with critical theory, which is concerned with the identification of power imbalances and the structures that create them. AI encourages participants to discuss the positive aspects of their work. Reason (2000) argues that AI, in trying to focus on the aspects of the organisation that work well, faces the danger that it will 'ignore the shadow' – that is, the realities of the working environment are ignored. The interviews with custody sergeants showed that this was not the case in this study. The officers involved did highlight aspects of good practice – for example, inter-agency working – but they were also very forthright in their discussion of perceived organisational and managerial failings. Police organisational culture, particularly its gallows humour, means that there was little likelihood, if any, that the more negative aspects of the process would be ignored in these interviews.

Two further studies went on to examine incidents of self-harm and the police response, and the assessment of mental health problems in the custody setting. Taken together, these constitute a case analysis of the sergeant's role in the management of mental illness and self-harm within the custody setting. Yin (1984, p 23) describes a case study as 'an empirical inquiry that investigates a contemporary phenomenon within its real-life context'. This can involve a longitudinal study of a single case, but this is not necessarily so. In this instance, it was a question of exploring – via interviews with custody sergeants, notes on individual custody records and police officers' short summaries of incidents of self-harm – police responses towards detained persons who were experiencing acute mental distress while in custody.

Yin (1984) outlines three types of case study: exploratory, descriptive and explanatory. McDonough and McDonough (1997) add interpretive and evaluative. Strake (1995) has three forms of case study: intrinsic (the specific problems of an individual case); instrumental (the study of a small group of cases); and collective (which involves the use of a number of sources). This work is an interpretive case study, which examines the custody sergeant's role in the assessment and subsequent management of mental distress. It involves the consideration of the wider socio-legal framework, including the Police and Criminal Evidence Act (PACE) 2004 and the MHA (1983), and also broader questions about the development of community-based mental health services. This work highlights the processes that have resulted in the CJS becoming a default provider of mental health care.

The strength of the case study approach lies in the ability to examine data within the context in which it is generated and used. The complexities of assessment and the management of detained persons could not be adequately explored by other methods (for example, surveys or questionnaires). Case studies allow for the examination of the contextual realities of the area being studied. They also allow for the uses of multiple sources of evidence. Denzin and Lincoln (1994) term this process 'triangulation', whereby the researcher examines different aspects of the social reality. This means that there is the possibility to explore the gap between what should or is meant to happen, and the organisational reality. A case study is not intended as a study of the whole organisation (Yin, 1984); this work is a consideration of only one aspect of policing and mental illness. In that sense, it is an examination at a micro rather than a macro level. The criticisms of case study approaches echo the wider ones of post-positivism (Bryman, 2012). These focus on an alleged lack of rigour and the problem of whether the results are generalisable (Jones and Mason, 2002; Neumann, 2013). These questions need to be recast depending on the claims made of the research. This work acknowledges that custody is a dynamic setting, where wider issues of welfare and justice are played out. Within that framework, it seeks to explore the factors that influence how custody sergeants carry out their role.

From this base, I began to examine broader issues across the CJS. Several key themes emerged here: the increased demand for mental health services in the CJS; the lack of training for police and prison staff; the marginalisation of women and those from black and minority ethnic (BME) groups; and the risk of self-harm and suicide.

Bourdieu's bureaucratic field and habitus

The research uses Chan's (1996) application of Pierre Bourdieu's notions of *bureaucratic field* and *habitus* to policing to explore the impact of mass incarceration and deinstitutionalisation. Chan argues that Bourdieu's theoretical approach emphasises the active role that police officers play in the application of policing skills in a particular social and political context. It thus forces researchers to acknowledge that there are multiple organisational cultures, since officers in different positions within the force will work under a different field or 'habitus'. In the research undertaken in custody settings, particularly in the interviews with custody sergeants, their perception of the role revealed a number of factors that influenced their attitudes and the development of a habitus.

The socio-legal and political context

Neo-liberalism

Since the mid-1970s, neo-liberal ideas have dominated economic policy. Even during the post-war boom and the wider application of Keynesian economics, there were those, such as Hayek (2001), who argued that the State's role was too large. Friedman (2002) and the Chicago School became increasingly influential following the OPEC crisis of 1973.

Neo-liberalism seeks to apply what it regards as the discipline of the market to as broad an area of life as possible. For neo-liberals, the market is the most efficient way to organise the provision of goods and services. This approach, it is argued, can be applied to areas such as health, education and welfare. These areas of social goods are regarded in social democratic models as the realm of the State. In the neo-liberal economic model the role of the State, as outlined in Nozick's *State, Anarchy and Utopia* (1974), is as a 'night-watchman' providing a framework for the market to function via legally enforceable contracts. Nozick argued that if the State strayed from this role, then it would inevitably lead to a loss of liberty for individuals. Liberty is a key value in this philosophical approach; in this context, liberty is best understood as freedom from government or other interference.

Neo-liberalism has influenced political programmes across the world. One of the key features has been the privatisation of previously State-held assets – for example, the Thatcher Government in the UK sold council housing and utilities (Gilmour, 1992). Alongside the sale of assets, neo-liberalism is committed to the deregulation of the market. The argument here is that State interference inevitably makes the market inefficient; therefore, a whole raft of protections for workers has been removed. As Garland (2001) notes, there is a paradox at the heart of late modernity: mechanisms of audit and surveillance have generally expanded in all areas apart from one – the market. Giroux (2011) argues that neo-liberalism has reduced the realm of democratic politics to market forces, or to market dominance, so that values outside of it become much less influential.

Bauman (2007) suggests that the result is the creation of a form of hyper-individualism. These charges have broad significance for the role of social work. One of the myths of social work is that all practitioners share essentially the same set of progressive social and political values. I have worked with social workers who hold a range of views, but what they all have in common is a commitment to social justice and trying to improve the lives of individuals. As Garrett (2013) argues, social work has always had a dual role – part social control and part emancipatory. Hall et al (2013) very presciently argued that the Left's response to neo-liberalism was likely to be a form of 'authoritarian populism'. This has certainly been the case in the UK where New Labour, followed by the Coalition, has introduced a series of measures in welfare and penal policy that are essentially modern versions of the 'less eligibility' policy. As the balance in social policy has shifted, the emphasis in social work has moved towards a focus on the social control aspects of the role. This can be seen in mental health services (Cummins, 2012) and child protection (Garrett, 2007). Since 2010 and the introduction of policies of austerity, it has been even more difficult for social workers in this area. Bourdieu (1998) characterised welfare and social control as the left and right hands of the State. There has been a shift in the role of social work from a supportive role to a more bureaucratised form of practice – focusing on risk management. Wacquant (2009a) describes these recent shifts in the balance between these two poles as a move from the protective to the disciplinary.

The penal state

The expansion of the use of imprisonment has been a feature of a number of jurisdictions. The USA has led the way in this penal arms race. Simon (2014a) identifies three elemental phases in the development of mass incarceration. Driven by a fear of crime and the political fallout from being seen as weak on the issues (Simon, 2007), prosecutors ask for custodial sentences where previously a community penalty would have been imposed. Then, sentences are increased – the war on drugs is an example of this process. Finally, mandatory and/or indeterminate sentences are introduced. These factors combine to produce a perfect storm. Simon demonstrates how law and order have come to dominate the structure of political debate, in ways that entrench the expansion of imprisonment. Progressive parties have been unable or unwilling to shift the terms of the debate for fear of being seen as soft on crime: being 'weak on crime' was viewed by strategists as political suicide. The Clinton and Blair administrations are excellent examples of progressive parties presiding over the expansion of the use of imprisonment.

Incarceration across the world

In Europe, the UK has been the country that has most closely followed the USA in its race to incarcerate. The statistics are astonishing, particularly when one considers that in the early 1970s, some sociologists were predicting the end of the prison as an institution. Walmsley (2013) provides a detailed analysis of rates of imprisonment across the world. As he notes, there are now 10.2 million people who are held in penal institutions; nearly a quarter of these prisoners – 2.4 million – are in prison in the USA. Along with Russia (0.68 million) and China (1.64 million), the USA holds nearly half the world's prisoners. Walmsley concludes that prison populations have been growing across all five continents over the past 15 years of the publication of the World Prison Population List. The standard comparative measure for imprisonment is the rate per 100,000 of the population. Since 1999, the overall world prison population rate has increased from 136 per 100,000 to 144 per 100,000. The USA remains at the top of this incarceration league with a rate of 716 per 100,000 (see www.prisonstudies.org/world-prison-brief for further details).

American exceptionalism

At the time of writing, Barack Obama has just become the first president to visit a federal prison. It appears that the use of imprisonment might become an election issue. Candidates from both Republican and Democratic parties have begun to talk openly about the need to reduce the use of imprisonment. Carson and Golinelli's (2013) analysis shows that the five states with highest imprisonment rates – Louisiana (1720), Mississippi (1370), Alabama (1234), Oklahoma (1178) and Texas (1121) – have rates that are well above the national average. The racial disparities in imprisonment are of equal concern, as the authors conclude:

> More than 60% of the people in prison today are people of color. Black men are six times more likely to be incarcerated than white men and 2.5 times more likely than Hispanic men. For black men in their thirties, 1 in every 10 is in prison or jail on any given day.
>
> (Carson and Golinelli, 2013, p 23)

The impact of imprisonment is not restricted to the individuals involved. There is a significant body of research that demonstrates the wider damage that has been done to the African-American community (Mauer, 2006; Clear, 2009; Drucker, 2011). The damage does not end when individuals are released. Many US states prevent ex-prisoners from voting, accessing social housing or completing educational programmes. Alexander (2012) powerfully argues that the overall effect serves to create a new 'caste' of disenfranchised and marginalised young black men.

Comparing penal regimes

Lacey (2008) warns against the dangers of making comparisons between penal regimes that ignore the wider cultural forces that contribute to the development of the cultures that underpin them. For example, she suggests that liberal market economies with the concomitant deeply engrained individualism have become more punitive. The USA is, of course, the prime example of this. However, as noted above, there are very significant variations between the states. When exploring penal policy, it is impossible to ignore the role of historical, social and other factors. When examining the European experiences of the expansion of imprisonment, Lacey's warning is just as important. Cavadino and Dignan (2006), in their analysis of penal policies and the use of imprisonment, developed a political economy typology: neo-liberal, conservative corporatist, social democratic and oriental corporatist. Examples of all these, apart from oriental corporatism, exist within Europe and the European Union.

Table I.1 highlights the differences in the uses of imprisonment between the countries of the European Union in the period 2003–12. The Baltic states have the highest rates of imprisonment. One might expect that these rates would decline as the shift towards democracy is strengthened and civil society becomes more established. Other local factors need to be considered; for example, Portugal's liberalisation of drug laws has led to a reduction in the use of imprisonment. The UK, Spain and France are examples where imprisonment has been on an upward curve and seems set to continue in that fashion. Germany and Holland are notable as countries where the use of imprisonment has fallen. Subramanian and Shames (2013) show that this is due to policies such as the concentrated use of community penalties and suspended sentences in both countries. Downes and Hansen's (2006) analysis of 18 countries, including the UK and the USA, concluded that there was a clear relationship between welfare provision and penal policy: the lower the spending on welfare, the higher the rate of imprisonment.

Table I.1 *European prison populations 2003–12*

Prison population
Last update: 27.02.15
Source of data: Eurostat

UNIT: Number

TIME GEO	2003	2004	2005	2006	2007	2008	2009	2010	2011	2012
Belgium	9,308	9,249	9,330	9,573	9,950	9,804	10,105	10,968	11,065	11,212
Bulgaria	10,056	10,935	11,399	11,452	10,792	9,922	9,167	9,429	9,885	9,904
Czech Republic	17,180	18,303	19,003	18,904	19,110	20,471	22,021	21,987	23,062	23,112
Denmark	3,641	3,767	4,041	3,932	3,646	3,530	3,715	3,965	4,037	3,984
Germany (until 1990 former territory of the FRG)	79,183	79,329	79,519	77,166	73,319	73,203	72,043	70,103	69,371	65,722
Estonia	4,352	4,575	4,410	4,310	3,466	3,656	3,555	3,393	3,400	3,286
Ireland	2,986	3,138	3,151	3,191	3,321	3,544	3,275	3,556	3,610	3,789
Greece	8,555	8,760	9,871	10,280	11,255	12,315	11,474	12,590	12,349	12,479
Spain	56,096	59,375	61,054	64,021	67,100	73,558	76,079	73,929	70,472	68,597
France	55,407	59,245	59,197	59,522	60,403	64,003	66,178	66,532	66,675	73,780
Croatia	2,803	3,010	3,485	3,833	4,290	4,734	4,891	5,165	5,064	4,741
Italy	54,237	56,068	59,523	39,005	48,693	58,127	64,791	67,961	66,897	65,701
Cyprus	355	546	536	599	646	646	670	637	634	694
Latvia	8,222	7,666	6,998	6,636	6,548	6,873	7,055	6,780	6,561	6,117
Lithuania	8,957	7,838	7,951	7,982	7,770	7,736	8,332	8,844	9,526	9,868
Luxembourg	455	577	735	738	666	674	679	669	632	633
Hungary	16,507	16,543	15,720	14,740	14,743	14,626	15,253	16,328	17,210	17,179
Malta	278	298	294	375	382	662	494	598	597	585
Netherlands	15,189	17,376	17,860	16,536	15,540	14,610	14,365	14,370	13,970	13,481
Austria	7,816	9,000	8,955	8,780	8,887	7,899	8,423	8,597	8,767	5,756
Poland	80,692	79,344	82,656	87,669	90,199	84,549	85,598	81,094	81,544	84,129
Portugal	13,635	12,956	12,687	12,446	11,587	10,807	11,099	11,613	12,681	13,614
Romania	42,815	39,031	36,700	34,038	29,390	26,212	26,716	28,244	30,694	31,817
Slovenia	1,099	1,126	1,132	1,127	1,336	1,318	1,360	1,351	1,273	1,377
Slovakia	8,829	9,504	9,289	8,657	8,235	8,313	9,033	10,068	10,713	11,075
Finland	3,463	3,535	3,883	3,477	3,370	3,457	3,231	3,189	3,261	3,196
Sweden	6,726	7,291	7,016	7,151	6,740	6,806	6,976	6,891	6,716	6,413
England and Wales	73,657	74,488	79,190	77,982	79,734	83,194	83,454	85,002	85,374	86,048
Scotland	6,606	6,776	6,856	7,187	7,376	7,826	7,963	7,853	8,178	:
Northern Ireland (UK)	1,128	1,219	1,325	1,501	1,484	1,490	1,465	1,469	1,703	1,742
Iceland	112	115	119	119	115	140	148	165	148	153
Liechtenstein	67	59	62	48	38	78	149	76	87	75
Norway	2,944	3,028	3,124	3,250	3,420	3,387	3,403	3,624	3,727	:
Switzerland	5,214	5,977	6,137	5,888	5,715	5,780	6,084	6,181	6,065	6,599
Montenegro	744	802	816	852	961	1,255	1,465	1,457	1,328	1,453
Former Yugoslav Republic of Macedonia, the	1,545	1,791	2,081	2,090	2,050	2,235	:	:	:	:
Serbia	7,128	7,653	8,078	7,862	8,970	9,701	10,795	11,211	11,094	10,226
Turkey	63,796	58,016	55,966	70,524	90,732	103,435	115,920	120,194	128,253	:
Bosnia and Herzegovina	:	:	:	:	:	:	:	:	12,763	:

Social work, Advanced Marginality and the CJS

Governing through crime

One of the most striking features of a number of modern democracies – particularly the USA but also the UK – is the expansion of the penal and criminal justice systems. Jonathan Simon (2007) sees these trends as coming together to create a new political meme which he calls 'Governing through Crime'. The main features of this new culture include: an increased concern with personal safety and responses, such as living in gated communities and driving SUVs – which provide a sense of security for the middle class – and the importance of individual high profile cases. For example, the brutal abduction and murder of Polly Klass in California in 1993 was followed by a campaign that led to the introduction of the 'three strikes law' in 1994. This law sentences offenders who have been convicted of a third felony to life imprisonment. This trend in political culture can be identified across a number of democracies, but the UK has followed the US trajectory most closely – both in terms of the increase in the use of imprisonment and also the wider discourse that demonises offenders, whatever the nature of their offence. The modern version of the spectacle of the scaffold is a seemingly endless succession of fly-on-the-wall documentaries that portray the poor as feckless, idle and a drain on stretched state resources. 'Poverty porn', such as Channel 4's *Benefits Street*, does not necessarily directly concern itself with the CJS but is part of a subtext: a number of individuals shown have been in Court; the state institutions have gone soft and can no longer effectively manage the poor; and so on. The idea that the CJS has gone soft appears to be a consistent feature of public debates on these issues. It has not lost any of its traction despite the exponential growth in imprisonment and the deteriorating conditions in prisons in England and Wales.

Wacquant (2008; 2009b; 2009c) argues that the growth of social insecurity and the expansion of the penal state are key features of the neo-liberal political project. Wacquant is particularly scathing of the role of think tanks in the spreading of the 'doxa' of the penal state, such as 'prison works', 'zero tolerance' and 'broken windows'. He outlines the ways in which these ideas have spread across the Atlantic. They have become key features of the development of a range of social policies in the UK. The Blair Government in particular adopted these ideas with enthusiasm in a raft of policies including, for example, anti-social behaviour orders (ASBOs). Wacquant throughout his work identifies the ways in which the *rehabilitative ideal* (Garland, 2001) – that is, the belief that offenders can change and it was a proper role of the State to assist this process – has all but disappeared. It has been replaced by a focus on risk and risk management. As Garland (2001) argues, offenders have moved from being considered fellow citizens in need of support to having rehabilitated themselves into sites of risk. As Beck (1992) notes, risk and risk management have become key societal themes which structure and lead public policy. Wacquant (2008) argues that the police, Courts and prisons now represent 'a core political capacity through which the state both produces and manages inequality, identity and marginality'. In this regard, Wacquant stands somewhat apart from other contemporary analysts of the expansion of the penal system. He argues that it is one of the core components of neo-liberalism.

The wider role of social work

Social work as a profession very much identifies itself as part of what Bourdieu termed the 'left hand' of the State (Garrett, 2007) – that is, those aspects of State services such as health and education broadly associated with the welfare of citizens. However, this value base has been systematically attacked and undermined in the UK. There are a number of policy initiatives which impact on social work that reflect this shift. For example, in the UK, the Troubled Families Agenda defines such families as follows: 'Troubled families are house-holds who: are involved in crime and anti-social behaviour, have children not in school, have an adult on out of work benefits and cause high costs to the public purse.' At the time of the introduction of this policy in 2012, the UK Government claimed that there were 120,000 such families and solving their problems would save £9 billion a year. Both these figures are not supported by any real evidence. However, of more significance is the fact that the agenda was introduced at the same time as changes to the benefits system most likely to impact on families in this group; for example, a cap on housing benefits payments was introduced. This meant that families claiming housing benefit, which is paid to landlords, in areas where the average rents were high – particularly London – would be moved to areas where rents were cheaper. In addition, such policies ignore those families under pressure that have not been defined as 'troubled'. The impact of poverty and austerity clearly has the potential to undermine any constructive work with such families. It is harder to get your children to school 'ready to learn' if you are living in overcrowded accommodation and reliant on food banks to feed them. The Troubled Families Agenda brings together several themes of neo-liberal social policy – the need to reduce public expenditure at the same time as making moral statements about the status of those subject to them

In setting out an agenda for a re-engaged progressive social work the Social Work Action Network (SWAN) produced a manifesto in 2004, arguing that the impact of neo-liberal social policies has highlighted that 'social work has to be defined not by its function for the state but by its value base'. This is a call for a return to social work based on the development of genuine personal relationships. This is far removed from the bureaucratic model that not only de-professionalises social work but also results in poor service outcomes. I have a great deal of sympathy with the broad thrust of such an approach, arguing that the CJS should be a key site for social work intervention.

Social work and poverty

Sociologists such as Tyler (*Revolting Subjects*, 2013), Slater (*The Myth of Broken Britain*, 2012) and Wacquant have examined the ways in which marginalised neighbourhoods and their citizens have become both physically and psychologically cut off from the wider society. This is a direct result of a range of economic and social policies that Wacquant terms 'crim-inalisation of poverty'. In *Prisons of Poverty* (2009) he outlines the development of 'a new government of social insecurity wedding the "invisible hand" of the deregulated labor market to the "iron fist" of an intrusive and omnipresent punitive apparatus'. His work shows the ways in which neo-liberal economic policies impact on the social structures of urban commu-nities. Existing networks of social capital have come under tremendous pressure as society becomes more atomised. A kcy mantra of Thatcherism was that it would lead to the 'rolling back of the State' (Gilmour, 1992). This should be understood not only as the removal of the State from areas of economic activity, but also the introduction of market forces into social welfare. Wacquant's work explores the ways in which the role of the 'night-watchman' State, in managing the working class and the poor, has been expanded and aggressively strengthened under neo-liberalism. This is part of a wider discourse, with its roots in Murray's (1990) underclass hypothesis that constructs the poor in eugenicist terms (Slater, 2012). Tyler (2013, p 38) explores the way that this 'hygienic governmentality' was reflected in Nicolas Sarkozy's comment that the young residents of the *banlieues* were *racaille* ('scum') that needed to be washed away with a 'Kärcher' – a high pressure cleaner. In her analysis of the response to the 2011 UK riots, Tyler (2013) shows the ways in which those involved were portrayed as vermin. Wacquant's work, in particular, demonstrates the linkages in this shift from a 'war on poverty' to a 'war on the poor'.

Why social work should play a wider role in the CJS

Social work and social workers inevitably are drawn into the retrenchment of welfare provision. They have a key role as gatekeepers. These processes are often at odds with the expressed value base of the profession. The expansion of imprisonment has a corrosive impact on not just individuals, but also communities. Social workers can contribute to the development of social networks and other forms of social capital working alongside individuals and communities. As a profession, it can take a leading role in the process of highlighting the damaging impact of current penal policies. One of the problems that the profession has consistently faced is a failure to explain to the wider public its role in providing support to vulnerable people and families. This has left it open to a series of lazy stereotypes, such as the radical politically correct social worker who is detached from the reality of the day-to-day lives of service users. Unfortunately, the profession still struggles to get this basic message across. This is demonstrated on a fairly regular basis in the media reporting of social workers' involvement in a host of issues, but particularly when reporting child protection failures (Jones, 2014).

The CJS should be a key concern for social work and social workers. This seems to me a statement of the obvious. It is an indication of the way that social work, as a profession, has lost its sense of purpose that I feel it necessary to state this. The probation service in England and Wales has been butchered. The idea that offenders need support, advice and help to rebuild their lives has become so marginalised that it appears almost like a 1970s fashion – popular at the time, but now the source of wider bemusement or embarrassment. However, all fashions come back into style. There are some indications that the mood is changing. There are cracks in the law-and-order/mass-imprisonment policy edifice. These are explored in more depth later. Social work as a profession needs to be more heavily involved in the process of pushing back the penal state – this book seeks to make a small contribution to this process.

The International Federation of Social Workers (IFSW) defines social work as:

> *a practice-based profession and an academic discipline that promotes social change and development, social cohesion, and the empowerment and liberation of people. Principles of social justice, human rights, collective responsibility and respect for diversities are central to social work. Underpinned by theories of social work, social sciences, humanities and indigenous knowledge, social work engages people and structures to address life challenges and enhance wellbeing.*
> (ifsw.org/policies/definition-of-social-work/)

I see this as a clear argument, but also a demand, that social work engages with all those in contact with the CJS – particularly those experiencing mental distress.

The Professional Capabilities Framework (PCF)

The PCF was developed by the Social Work Reform Board as part of the review of the profession following the death of Baby P. The PCF is an overarching framework which outlines the professional standards that social workers should maintain and it applies to all social workers in England. There are nine domains with different levels of expectation for each stage of a social worker's career (see Figure I.1). These domains are further outlined in Table I.2.

I argue that, alongside the new duties that the Care Act creates, the PCF can be read as further support for social work re-engaging with the CJS. The domains of 'diversity' and 'rights, justice and economic well-being' are ones that are of particular importance in this field.

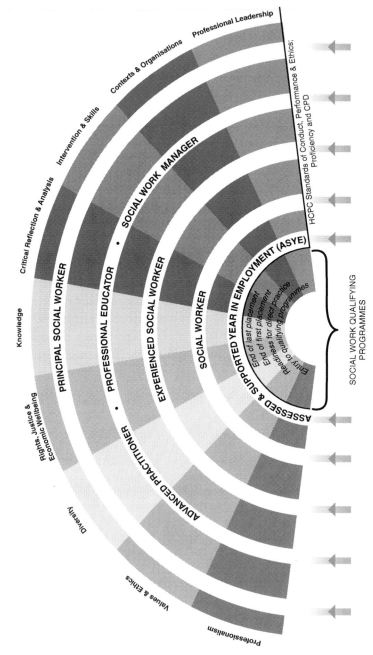

Figure I.1. The Professional Capabilities Framework (from www.basw.co.uk/resource/?id=1137)

Table I.2 Domains of the PCF

Domain	Outline
PROFESSIONALISM	Identify and behave as a professional social worker, committed to professional development. Social workers are members of an internationally recognised profession, a title protected in UK law. Social workers demonstrate professional commitment by taking responsibility for their conduct, practice and learning, with support through supervision. As representatives of the social work profession they safeguard its reputation and are accountable to the professional regulator.
VALUES AND ETHICS	Apply social work ethical principles and values to guide professional practice. Social workers have an obligation to conduct themselves ethically and to engage in ethical decision making, including through partnership with people who use their services. Social workers are knowledgeable about the value base of their profession, its ethical standards and relevant law.
DIVERSITY	Recognise diversity and apply anti-discriminatory and anti-oppressive principles in practice. Social workers understand that diversity characterises and shapes human experience and is critical to the formation of identity. Diversity is multidimensional and includes race, disability, class, economic status, age, sexuality, gender and transgender, faith and belief. Social workers appreciate that, as a consequence of difference, a person's life experience may include oppression, marginalisation and alienation as well as privilege, power and acclaim, and are able to challenge appropriately.
RIGHTS, JUSTICE AND ECONOMIC WELL-BEING	Advance human rights and promote social justice and economic well-being. Social workers recognise the fundamental principles of human rights and equality, and that these are protected in national and international law, conventions and policies. They ensure these principles underpin their practice. Social workers understand the importance of using and contributing to case law and applying these rights in their own practice. They understand the effects of oppression, discrimination and poverty.
KNOWLEDGE	Apply knowledge of social sciences, law and social work practice theory. Social workers understand psychological, social, cultural, spiritual and physical influences on people; human development throughout the life-span and the legal framework for practice. They apply this knowledge in their work with individuals, families and communities. They know and use theories and methods of social work practice.

Table I.2 (cont.)

Domain	Outline
CRITICAL REFLECTION AND ANALYSIS	Apply critical reflection and analysis to inform and provide a rationale for professional decision making. Social workers are knowledgeable about and apply the principles of critical thinking and reasoned discernment. They identify, distinguish, evaluate and integrate multiple sources of knowledge and evidence. These include practice evidence, their own practice experience, service user and carer experience together with research-based, organisational, policy and legal knowledge. They use critical thinking augmented by creativity and curiosity.
INTERVENTION AND SKILLS	Use judgement and authority to intervene with individuals, families and communities to promote independence, provide support and prevent harm, neglect and abuse. Social workers engage with individuals, families, groups and communities, working alongside people to assess and intervene. They enable effective relationships and are effective communicators, using appropriate skills. Using their professional judgement, they employ a range of interventions: promoting independence, providing support and protection, taking preventative action and ensuring safety while balancing rights and risks. They understand and take account of differentials in power, and are able to use authority appropriately. They evaluate their own practice and the outcomes for those with whom they work.
CONTEXTS AND ORGANISATIONS	Engage with, inform and adapt to changing contexts that shape practice. Operate effectively within own organisational frameworks and contribute to the development of services and organisations. Operate effectively within multi-agency and interprofessional settings. Social workers are informed about and are pro-actively responsive to the challenges and opportunities that come with changing social contexts and constructs. They fulfil this responsibility in accordance with their professional values and ethics, both as individual professionals and as members of the organisation in which they work. They collaborate, inform and are informed by their work with others, interprofessionally and with communities.
PROFESSIONAL LEADERSHIP	Take responsibility for the professional learning and development of others through supervision, mentoring, assessing, research, teaching, leadership and management. The social work profession evolves through the contribution of its members in activities such as practice research, supervision, assessment of practice, teaching and management. An individual's contribution will gain influence when undertaken as part of a learning, practice-focused organisation. Learning may be facilitated with a wide range of people, including social work colleagues, service users and carers, volunteers, foster carers and other professionals.

Mental health social work

What is the contribution that social work can make in the broad field of mental health, including services within the CJS? The World Health Organization (WHO) updated its definition of mental health in August 2014 to mean:

> a state of wellbeing in which the individual realises his or her own abilities, can cope with the normal stresses of life, can work productively and fruitfully, and is able to make a contribution to his or her community.
>
> (www.who.int/features/factfiles/mental_health/en)

Mental health is an interdisciplinary field and needs to be approached in this fashion. A new model needs to be developed that takes proper account of the wide range of factors that contribute to the development and impact of mental illness. In particular, it is important that mental health services work in much more meaningful ways with service users. The IFSW definition of social work can act as the starting point here. Mental health services have a history that is scarred by the appalling treatment of individuals and minorities (Scull, 2015). Social work needs to accept that it is part of this history; to acknowledge this history does not mean that we have to be trapped by it.

Social work finds itself in an ambiguous position in the mental health field. The Approved Mental Health Professional (AMHP) role is still overwhelmingly carried out by social workers. This means that there is a focus on assessment and the use of detention. However, at the same time, policy developments such as personalisation and legislation, including the Care Act (2014) and Social Services and Well-being (Wales) Act 2014, mean that there is a greater emphasis than ever on individuals' social networks to meet their own care needs. These developments alongside a renewed interest in the recovery model as an approach offer the chance of a revitalised model of social work practice – one that casts aside the dead hand of managerialism and risk assessment that have been the strongest drivers of service and practice development for too long. Social work, with its commitment to individuals and the development of wider community resources and social capital, has a key role to play.

Taking it further

Backwith, D (2015) *Social Work, Poverty and Exclusion*. Maidenhead: Open University Press.

Foucault, M (2006) *The History of Madness*. Abingdon: Routledge.

Friedman, M (2002) *Capitalism and Freedom* (40th anniversary edition). London: University of Chicago Press.

Garland, D (2001) *The Culture of Control: Crime and Social Order in Contemporary Society*. Chicago: University of Chicago Press.

Garrett, P M (2013) *Social Work and Social Theory: Making Connections*. Bristol: Policy Press.

Hayek, F (2001) *The Road to Serfdom* (Routledge Classics). London: Routledge.

Jones, R (2014) *The Story of Baby P: Setting the Record Straight*. Bristol: Policy Press.

Lacey, N (2008) *The Prisoner's Dilemma*. Cambridge: Cambridge University Press.

Neumann, L (2013) *Social Research Methods: Qualitative and Quantitative Approaches* (7th edition). London: Pearson.

Simon, J (2007) *Governing Through Crime: How the War on Crime Transformed American Democracy and Created a Culture of Fear*. Oxford: Oxford University Press.

Strake, R E (1995) *The Art of Case Study Research*. Thousand Oaks, CA: Sage.

SWAN (2004) Manifesto 2004 [online]. Available at: www.socialworkfuture.org (accessed 15 December 2015).

Tyler, I (2013) *Revolting Subjects: Social Abjection and Resistance in Neoliberal Britain*. London: Zed Books.

Wacquant, L (2009) *Punishing the Poor: The Neoliberal Government of Social Insecurity*. Durham, NC: Duke University Press.

1 Key Decision Points

Critical questions

- *Why is the term 'mentally disordered offender' so difficult to define?*
- *What potential risks do people with mental health problems face in the CJS?*
- *What special protections does the CJS afford people with mental health problems?*

In 1780 John Howard carried out his famous inspection of the state of the prisons in England. As well as describing the appalling physical conditions that led to disease and hunger, and the corruption among warders, Howard noted that the prisons were housing more 'idiots and lunatics'. Howard also argued that the increases in the number of what we would now term 'mentally disordered offenders' had a detrimental effect on the prison regime for all those in prison. There have been similar observations at a number of points since. One of the main themes of this book is that the policy of deinstitutionalisation, which has taken place during a period when the use of imprisonment has expanded, has exacerbated these problems. The CJS has become a default provider of mental health care. This is the case across all the stages – or what I term here the *key decision points* – of the CJS, and applies from the police officer on the beat to the prison estate.

Who are 'mentally disordered offenders'?

There is no widely agreed definition of this term. In this book, I use the term in the broadest sense, meaning 'anyone in contact with the CJS who has mental health problems'. This is a very wide definition and includes groups with varying needs. It will thus include acutely unwell individuals, who might be admitted to a mental health unit, and also those who would be treated as an outpatient. It is important to note that the term is not limited to individuals who have committed an offence because of symptoms of mental illness. This is a relatively small, but obviously important, group and the wider definition forces us to examine these issues in greater depth.

Λ key theme of this book is that the mental health of an individual is a factor that can, and should, be a consideration in decision making at all points of the CJS. It is important to emphasise that the focus here is not on people with mental health problems who are victims of crime. In many of the situations covered here (for example, encountering a police officer on street patrol) there will not be a formal diagnosis – nor is one required. However, in the Courts and forensic services, there will be formal assessments by mental health professionals. The 2007 reform of the MHA removed the four categories that mental disorder had been divided into (*mental illness, psychopathic disorder, mental impairment* and *severe mental impairment*). Assessment is now simplified to a question of whether, in medical opinion, the person suffers from 'any disorder or disability of the mind'. There is a further distinction to be made here: patients who have learning disabilities are not 'mentally disordered' within the terms of the MHA, unless their behaviour is additionally regarded as 'abnormally aggressive or seriously irresponsible'.

Key decision points of the CJS

Goldberg and Huxley (1980) identified a series of filters to explain the relationship between rates of mental illness in the community and admission. They were exploring why mental health problems were often overlooked. In this model, contact with GPs was a key filter – if you do not see a doctor you are not going to be given a formal diagnosis. We then have to look at the experience of visiting a GP – some are better at identifying mental health problems; a patient with a very good relationship with their GP might be more able to disclose distressing symptoms and so on. Goldberg and Huxley's model also allows for the fact that the nature of the illness will have an impact; for example, an acutely psychotic patient is much more likely to be diagnosed than those from other groups.

A similar model can be applied in the CJS. At all stages of the CJS – from an encounter with a police officer on the street to sentencing at the Crown Court – the mental health of an individual can, and should, be a factor in the decision-making process. Table 1.1 looks at the major points of the system, outlining the policy, legislative framework and what I see as the key decision points for each stage. When using this approach, one also has to take account of the wider context. It is vital to recognise that the pressures within the CJS mean that many individuals who are experiencing mental distress are not identified at all, or only later in the system. The police, Courts and prisons can be viewed as a series of filters or potential decision points. The actual recognition is the result of a combination of factors including: the nature and presentation of the mental health issue; the environment in which the assessment takes place; and the experience and knowledge of the staff involved.

All these policies need to be viewed in the light of the *Mental Health Crisis Care Concordat* that was launched in 2014 (www.crisiscareconcordat.org.uk). This is a national statement of aims that will form the basis of local plans to ensure that those in crisis receive timely and appropriate treatment and support. There are four main areas:

- Access to support before crisis point – making sure people with mental health problems can get help 24 hours a day and that, when they ask for help, they are taken seriously.

- Urgent and emergency access to crisis care – making sure that a mental health crisis is treated with the same urgency as a physical health emergency.

- Quality of treatment and care when in crisis – making sure that people are treated with dignity and respect, in a therapeutic environment.

- Recovery and staying well – preventing future crises by making sure people are referred to appropriate services.

Table 1.1 Key decision points

Decision point	Areas to consider	Legislative and policy framework
Policing	As discussed in Chapter 5, day-to-day policing involves a great deal of mental health related work.	• National decision-making model • Street triage schemes • Section 136 MHA powers
Police custody	Custody officers have a key role in the assessment of vulnerable people. The custody environment can exacerbate mental health problems. People with mental health problems are widely recognised as being at particular risk in custody.	• PACE (2004) • Liaison and diversion schemes • The role of the forensic physician • Assessment by custody sergeants • The role of the appropriate adult • MHA assessments in custody
Prosecution	In all cases, including those where an offender has a mental illness, the Crown Prosecution Service has to decide whether: • there is evidence to secure a conviction; • a prosecution is in the public interest. The Crown Prosecution Service has to consider a range of factors, including the nature of the alleged offence, whether the individual is receiving treatment and community safety.	• Code for Crown Prosecutors • Home Office Circular 66/90 • Home Office Circular 12/95 • Joint Working Agreement between the Association of Chief Police Officers, the Crown Prosecution Service and NHS Protect • Diverting offenders with mental health problems and/or learning disabilities within the National Conditional Cautioning Framework (Crown Prosecution Service)

Table 1.1 *(cont.)*

Decision point	Areas to consider	Legislative and policy framework
The Courts	The majority of cases will be heard in the Magistrates' Court. More serious matters are taken afterwards to the Crown Court, and the remanded are sent to hospital for a report (section 35 MHA, 1983) or for treatment (section 36). In a very small number of cases, the issue arises as to whether the defendant is fit to plead. This issue is decided by the judge on the basis of two medical reports, one of which must come from a section 12 MHA approved doctor. The issue of mental state will also be considered in cases where defendants plead not guilty on the grounds of diminished responsibility.	• Criminal Procedure (Insanity) Act 1964 as amended by the Criminal Procedure (Insanity and Unfitness to Plead) Act 1991 • Section 35/36 MHA 1983 • Section 37 MHA • Liaison and diversion schemes based at Courts • Ministry of Justice (2008) *Guidance for the Courts on Remand and Sentencing Powers for Mentally Disordered Offenders*
Sentencing	Chapter 3 contains a full discussion of the philosophical and ethical issues raised here. It should be noted that the overwhelming majority with a mental health problem are not within specialist forensic services. The normal range of sentences are thus open to the Courts. However, there are important mental health options, including: • Mental Health Treatment Requirement (MHTR), which is available to the Courts as a sentencing option for community orders. These orders have rarely been used. • Section 37 MHA – *hospital order.* The purpose of the order is to divert offenders to psychiatric care. Without the addition of restrictions, it has the same effect as section 3.	• Code for Crown Prosecutors • Ministry of Justice (2008) *Guidance for the Courts on Remand and Sentencing Powers for Mentally Disordered Offenders* • National Offender Management Service: *Supporting Community Order Treatment Requirements* • Section 207 of the Criminal Justice Act 2003 creates MHRT • Section 37 MHA • Section 41 MHA • Section 45A MHA • Ministry of Justice – Mental Health Casework Section • Ministry of Justice (2009) *Guidance for Social Supervisors* • Ministry of Justice (2010) *Guidance for Working with MAPPA and Mentally Disordered Offenders*

Table 1.1 (cont.)

Decision point	Areas to consider	Legislative and policy framework
	• Section 41 – *restriction order.* This is imposed where the Court feels that it is 'necessary for the protection of the public from serious harm'. The impact is that the patient can only be given leave, transferred to a different hospital or discharged with the agreement of the Secretary of State. • This group of patients – 37/41 – are usually admitted to secure units or to special hospitals. These patients are subject to social supervision when they are discharged. They are also likely to be under the local multi-agency public protection arrangements (MAPPA) procedures. • Section 45A – *hybrid order.* The impact of such an order is essentially the same as section 37. However, under section 45A MHA, once treatment is no longer necessary, the offender continues to serve out the remainder of their sentence in a prison.	
Post-sentencing	Chapters 4 and 6 look at the needs of those with mental health problems in prison. The fundamental principle is outlined in the Trenčín Statement that prisoners should not be denied health care because of their status. This applies to both physical and mental health issues. As we have seen, the health care needs of prisoners are much greater than the wider population: • All prisoners are assessed on reception.	• Trenčín Statement on the treatment of prisoners (WHO 2007) • Section 47 and Section 48 MHA • Health Advisory Committee for the Prison Service (1997) *The Provision of Mental Health Care in Prisons* • HM Prison Service and NHS Executive (1999) *The Future Organisation of Prison Health Care* • Department of Health (2006) *Procedure for the Transfer of Prisoners to and from Hospital under Sections 47 and 48 of the MHA*

Table 1.1 *(cont.)*

Decision point	Areas to consider	Legislative and policy framework
	• Mental health inreach teams have been established to identify and support those prisoners with the greatest mental health needs. • Acutely ill prisoners can be transferred to forensic mental health services under section 47 or section 48 MHA.	• Department of Health and HM Prison Service (2001) *Changing the Outlook: A Strategy for Developing Mental Health Services in Prisons* • Department of Health and National Institute for Mental Health in England (2005) *Offender Mental Health Care Pathway*

Current key issues

In this section I will identify the current key issues in this field. They will be explored in more depth throughout the book.

The impact of austerity

In 2011 the Coalition Government published a new strategy for mental health services. The title, *No Health Without Mental Health*, is a clear statement of ambition. The document included six very clear objectives, which were to be the key for the development of mental health services:

- *more people will have good mental health;*
- *more people with mental health problems will recover;*
- *more people with mental health problems will have good physical health;*
- *more people will have a positive experience of care and support;*
- *fewer people will suffer avoidable harm;*
- *fewer people will experience stigma and discrimination.*
  (www.gov.uk/government/publications/the-mental-health-strategy-for-england)

This is a broad perspective on mental health that moves away from a focus on institutionalised forms of care. Unfortunately, the optimism of that statement has not been maintained. As Beresford (2013) notes, mental health services have reached a crisis point. The impact of austerity is twofold. First, there is a reduction in service provision as funding for statutory, voluntary and third sector services is cut. This is coupled with the social and psychological consequences of the impact of austerity on individuals and communities. A rise in suicides is a phenomenon in periods of austerity or economic difficulties, such as what we are going through now. However, people with mental health problems can face a number of additional difficulties. The changes to the benefit system, in particular the assessment of an individual's capability at work, are producing further pressures.

The 'invisibility' and fluctuating nature of mental health problems can also make it very difficult for individuals and carers to document adequately – that is, to the satisfaction of the assessors – the impact that mental illness has on their day-to-day lives. This produces a situation where an individual is assessed as 'fit for work' but can't find employment because of discrimination and stereotypical attitudes.

The role of the police

Lord Adebowale (2013) described mental health as 'core business' for the police. His study confirmed earlier work by the Sainsbury Centre for Mental Health (2009), which concluded that between 15% and 20% of police work relates to mental health issues. A very significant proportion of this work involves dealing with cases where people with mental health problems are victims of crime. To this must be added cases where people with mental health problems have committed crimes, mental health emergencies and section 136 MHA, supporting community mental health services and ensuring that people in custody are safe. One of my main arguments throughout this book is that the collapse of community mental health provision has increased the pressures on the police in this area.

The experiences of marginalised groups in the CJS

In 2010, as part of the general election, a group of campaigning organisations, charities and voluntary agencies produced the *Black Manifesto*. The aim of the document was to outline the extent of discrimination and racism that black citizens faced, including in all public services. Both the CJS and mental health services have histories that are scarred by their treatment of racial minorities, women and gay men and lesbians. Despite some progress and changes in social attitudes, it would be naive to think that BME groups do not face discrimination within the CJS. The Corston Inquiry (2007) examined the need for a rethink in attitudes to female offenders, particularly the need to focus on community-based alternatives to imprisonment.

The state of prisons in England and Wales in 2015

It is a shock to think that many of the factors that John Howard identified in 1780 are still with us today, perhaps in a slightly altered form. The huge increase in suicides in prison, along with violence and instances of poor care, demonstrate the sorry state of modern prisons. The latest 2013–14 annual report from the Chief Inspector of Prisons for England and Wales paints a very disturbing portrait of the current prison regime and makes for depressing reading. Chief Inspector Nick Hardwick's report showed there was a 69% rise in suicides in prison in 2013–14. He described it as 'the most unacceptable feature' of a prison system which is experiencing a 'rapid deterioration' in safety standards. Bullying, violence – including sexual violence – and intimidation are commonplace. The report also indicates that drugs are widely available, while there is often little constructive activity for prisoners in overcrowded institutions. The report describes unacceptable conditions in the following terms:

At its worst, overcrowding meant two prisoners sharing a six foot by ten foot cell designed for one, with bunks along one wall, a table and chair for one, some shelves, a small TV, an unscreened toilet at the foot of the bunks, little ventilation and a sheet as a makeshift curtain.

A few prisoners might spend 23 hours a day in such a cell. Twenty hours was relatively common in a local prison. Prisoners would eat most of their meals in their cell. The food budget was reduced from £2.20 per prisoner per day in 2012 to £1.96 a day in 2013.

(HM Chief Inspector of Prisons for England and Wales, 2014)

Rediscovering dignity: a social work perspective

In 1990, a response to a previous crisis in the prison system in England and Wales led to prison riots, including one at Strangeways Prison in Manchester, which was the longest in UK penal history. A public inquiry (Woolf, 1991) was conducted. The riots were a response to overcrowding and the poor conditions in prisons including the practice of 'slopping out' – where prisoners had to use buckets as a toilet and empty them out each morning. The practice was abolished in England as late as 1995. It should be noted that the prison population, at the time of the riots, was less than half what it is now.

The Woolf Report was seen as a blueprint for an improved prison system. The Home Office developed policies to reduce imprisonment on the basis that 'prison is an expensive way of making bad people worse'. These liberal moves were abandoned under new Home Secretary Michael Howard, who was committed to the idea that 'prison works' (Gottschalk, 2006). The result was a prison boom that continued under the New Labour administrations.

It is indicative of the current crisis that Lord Woolf has written the foreword to a recent report, *Presumption Against Imprisonment*, that calls for a radical rethink in penal policy. As Woolf argues: 'Imprisonment should not be the default sentence handed down. We should instead seek to develop a clear framework for identifying the kinds of case in which imprisonment will be the appropriate sentence.' To achieve this, the report recommends:

1. Using diversion from the courts more extensively
2. Promoting greater use of alternative forms of sentence
3. Prohibiting or restricting the imposition of short custodial sentences
4. Removing or restricting the sanction of imprisonment for certain offences
5. Reviewing sentence lengths
6. Removing mentally disordered and addicted persons from prisons.
        (www.britac.ac.uk/policy/Presumption_Against_Imprisonment.cfm)

Such policies chime with core social work values and are based on an implicit recognition of the inherent dignity of individuals. Social work needs to forcefully make the case that imprisonment fails on its own terms and has a devastating impact on individuals, families and communities. Rediscovering notions of dignity and developing policies based upon these is the place to start.

Taking it further

Adebowale, Lord (2013) *Independent Commission on Mental Health and Policing Report*. London: Independent Commission on Mental Health and Policing.

Beresford, P (2013) Mental Health is in No Fit State, Whatever the Politicians Say [online]. Available at: theconversation.com/mental-health-is-in-no-fit-state-whatever-the-politicians-say-15743 (accessed 15 December 2015).

Bradley, K (2009) *The Bradley Report: Lord Bradley's Review of People with Mental Health Problems or Learning Disabilities in the Criminal Justice System*: London: Department of Health.

HM Chief Inspector of Prisons for England and Wales (2014) *Annual Report 2013–14*. London: HMSO.

The Race Equality Centre (2010) *The Price of Race Inequality: The Black Manifesto 2010* [online]. Available at: www.theraceequalitycentre.org.uk/pdf/manifesto_summary4thApril.pdf (accessed 15 December 2015).

Seddon, T (2007) *Punishment and Madness*. Oxford: Routledge.

2 A Short History of Community Care

Critical questions

- *What were the key drivers of the development of community care?*
- *What are the links between the development of community care and the increase in the number of people with mental health problems in the CJS?*
- *Why was there a 'moral panic' about community care in the late 1980s and early 1990s?*

One of the key arguments of this book is that the collapse of community mental health services has led to the agencies of the CJS becoming key providers of mental health care. The boundaries between the two systems are not really as concrete as we imagine – Morabito (2007) describes them as 'porous'. I argue that, to understand the current situation, it is necessary to examine the roots of community care and its failure to be implemented properly. The progressive ideals of the opponents of institutionalised care chime with key social work notions – founded on the fundamental dignity and inherent worth of all individuals as fellow citizens. The danger is that the backlash against community care and the 'moral panic' of its reporting in the 1990s have marginalised these values.

The original notion of community care – properly resourced and community-based, to support citizens in acute distress – has been lost in a world of managerialist doublespeak and risk assessment. As Turner and Colombo (2008) argue, risk assessment has replaced an ethic of care as the main focus of service user contact. While I agree with the thrust of the argument here, I feel that there is a danger of a kind of therapeutic pessimism dominating these debates. There have always been practitioners who are very skilled at carving out a creative space in which to work alongside service users and their families. Social workers have traditionally placed tremendous value and importance on this as a way of maintaining professional integrity and identity (Morriss, 2014). One of the aims of this book is to contribute in a small way to a return to social work based on developing personal relationships and an emotional connection between workers and those experiencing distress. An understanding of the rise and fall of the asylums, the radical challenge to psychiatry and the subsequent failings of community care can be the start of this rebuilding process. It will allow us to see that the progressive values that influenced the development of community care continue to be relevant. In fact, in a world of austerity and the retrenchment of the welfare state, they are more vital than ever.

Penrose and the relationship between prisons and psychiatric care

Lionel Penrose (1939; 1943) put forward the intriguing hypothesis that there is a fluid relationship between the use of psychiatric inpatient beds and the use of custodial sentences. The 1939 paper was based on the analysis of statistics from European countries and argues that there was an inverse relationship between the provision of mental hospitals and the rate of serious crime in the countries studied – as one increases, the other decreases. The 1943 paper was a study of the rates of hospital admissions in different states in the USA and the numbers in state prisons. Later in his work, Penrose argued that a measurable index of the state of development of a country could be obtained by dividing the total number of people in mental hospitals and similar institutions by the number of people in prison. Penrose's work in this area concludes that society responds to challenging or bizarre behaviour in one of two ways – either by the use of the CJS or the mental health system. The system with the greater capacity at the time takes on this role.

Development of institutional care for the mentally ill

Pilgrim and Rogers (2013) suggest that the asylum is a hospital apart both physically and metaphorically from its general counterpart. The general hospital is easy to access and is usually found in the centre of towns and cities. The reverse is the case for the asylums. These institutions were built on sites away from the main centres of population, thus physically separating the 'mad' from the rest of the population. Scull (1977) sees the rise of asylums as part of the Victorian response to the problems of urbanisation. In this analysis, asylums – along with schools, factories and prisons – have a key role to play in social control. Scull argues that as the mad were deemed not to be economically useful, they had to be isolated and removed from society; the net effect was also to serve as a warning to the wider populace of the perils of non-conformity. In addition, this period saw the wider acceptance of a medical view of the causes of mental illness. The asylums, therefore, were the confirmation of the new status of psychiatry as a distinct branch of the medical profession.

Foucault's analysis: a brief summary

Foucault's (1991) analysis of the development of asylums and prisons has been incredibly influential. Foucault is concerned with the exercise of power, both by individuals and the State, and turns the Enlightenment idea of progress and the belief that social problems can be solved by rational means on their heads. In his work, both on prisons and asylums, Foucault argues that the development of these institutions represents an ideological shift. The focus for State intervention was no longer the bodies of prisoners or patients, but their minds. He argues that this is a more pervasive form of social control. In this analysis, power – and the power to punish – is much more dispersed throughout the social system; it therefore operates on a number of levels. Foucault terms this ideology of discipline *savoir*. Expressions of this ideology can be found among all groups, including those termed 'deviant', and it operates as a mechanism of repression, both of the self and others.

Foucault (1982) explores the way in which so-called 'dividing practices' operate. For Foucault, the subject is objectified by the process of being deemed 'mad', 'bad', 'sick' or 'healthy' and he argues that the 'Great Confinement' saw the development of institutionalisation as the response to the poor, mad or offenders. In *Discipline and Punish,* Foucault (1991) outlines the development of the 'disciplinary gaze', the process by which individuals become cases subject to a system of classification and control. These 'dividing practices' are the application of a branch of knowledge, such as psychiatry or criminology, that justifies the institutionalisation of the individual subject. The application of such knowledge, for Foucault, creates new groups or cases or, as he puts it, 'specifications of individuals'.

Seddon (2007), in his review of the treatment of mentally disordered offenders, concludes that prisons have always housed large numbers of the insane. For Seddon, this is not a recent development caused by the failings of community care; it is, rather, a fundamental feature of the prison as an institution. He highlights that there are strong links between the developments of the discourses of psychiatry and criminology. The two forms of discourse can often be said to be in competition; however, they also overlap. The competition is between professionals to exercise a dominant position in the policy debates. This clearly then has a whole range of implications for individual and professional status. For example, Seddon argues that there have been persistent attempts to establish links between madness and criminality in the case of women offenders, which have been the basis for developing special responses to women who offend. The Corston Inquiry (2007) is a recent response to this issue. The Inquiry was a response to a series of suicides and incidents of self-harm among female prisoners. It is striking how the report represents the needs of these women largely in terms of their mental health.

As with the more traditional Marxist analysis of Scull, Foucault argues that the development of these institutions is part of the strategy of the bourgeois response to the threat posed by the urban poor. For Foucault, the level of investment required in these institutions is such that if they did not serve this function, they would not have been built. In his writings, Foucault draws attention to the symbolism of the institutions. Bentham's Panopticon (Foucault, 1991) becomes not just an architectural design but an embodiment of new society, whose institutions form a 'carceral archipelago' for the management of deviant populations, be they criminals or the insane. Despite the persistent failure on an individual level of prisons or asylums to create model citizens, for Foucault, this was not the essential aim of such institutions; their fundamental role was the quarantining of the urban poor and they achieved this aim.

Response to the radical perspective on the rise of asylums

The accounts that Scull and Foucault give of the rise of the asylums can be seen as a response to the more traditional view that asylums, with all their faults, should be seen as progress on the way to a more enlightened treatment of the 'mad'. In this schema, the asylums were part of medical progress and the motives of the reformers were undoubtedly humanitarian and concerned with the relief of suffering (Jones, 1960). In this narrative of progress and reform, individuals such as the Tukes of York were seen as pursuing a heroic path in the face of hostility from wider society. The resulting institutions were attempts to provide safety and succour for the most vulnerable in society. In this account, the issue of social control is barely considered; similarly, for Scull or Foucault, there seems to be no acknowledgement that some reforms might have been the result of humanitarian concerns. The accounts given by Scull and Foucault are linked by a challenge to the Enlightenment view of rationality and progress. Both accounts take issue with the liberal view that sees the development of the asylum as part of a modernist, rational and technocratic response to social problems.

The liberal progressive view of the development of asylums is based on several key premises about the nature of mental illness and society. As Ignatieff (1985) argues, the orthodox view assumes that mental illness is an identifiable feature of the human condition. Following on from this basic premise is the idea that those who are involved in the management of mental health problems are motivated by humanitarian concerns for the relief of the distress of their fellow citizens. The final feature of this model is the acceptance of the dominant position of the medical profession in this process. This is seen as a logical outcome and allows for the application of rational, morally neutral medical knowledge to the symptoms of mental illness. The motor for change is a progressive impulse to find ways of improving services by the application of new knowledge. Rothman (1971) suggests this leads to a peculiar narrative, in which reformers design a new system, then expose the failings of the new system and eventually replace it with another one. In this account, there is a danger that historical development is seen as linear and teleological.

While there is clearly a range of critical perspectives on psychiatry (eg Foucault, 1991; Scull, 1977; Laing, 1959, 1967; Szasz, 1971), it should be noted that Szasz stands apart here. He is essentially a right-wing libertarian committed to a small State and he views mental illness as a form of social malingering – his views are neatly summed up in his 1995 paper 'Idleness and Lawlessness in the Therapeutic State'. Within the other perspectives, there are a range of views; however, a number of common themes can be identified. The first is a questioning of the assumption that mental illness exists in the way that psychiatrists and medicine suggest. In these critical accounts, there is a sceptical approach which sees mental illness as largely socially caused by the injustices of a capitalist society: poverty, racism, gender discrimination and social inequality. Mental illness is socially constructed; whereas treatment is seen as a therapeutic intervention in progressive accounts, from a critical perspective, it becomes part of the means by which capitalist society maintains social order and reproduces the class divisions required to ensure its continued existence.

For Scull (1977) the squalid conditions in the nineteenth-century asylums were inevitable. It would be impossible to think of an alternative as there was no system of welfare payments that existed to support these individuals. In addition, families often welcomed the removal of a non-contributing member as this reduced the burden on the family as whole. As Scull points out, most of urban society, apart from the ruling elite, lived a marginalised existence in very poor conditions indeed. In such circumstances, those who could not make any contribution would be seen as an economic danger. For Foucault (1991), the investment in the asylums was justified because of the role they played in social control and not because of the humanitarian zeal of the builders of these institutions. Both approaches argue that what later came to be seen as the failings of the asylums – cruelty, squalid living conditions and inhumane treatment – were, in fact, inherent features of their design. For example, while most commentators see the development of the Tuke Retreat at York as a progressive measure, Foucault (1982) essentially sees it as the exercise of power by other means. He describes the 'moralising sadism' of the Yorkshire Retreat and its Quaker founders. In Foucault's terms, the outcomes for the inmates are the same: exclusion and subjugation. Stone (1982) argues that there is a nihilism at the heart of Foucault's thinking that means that he sees all relationships in terms of power/subjugation. Stone concludes that this makes it impossible for Foucault to accept that there might have been a humanitarian root to the development of these institutions.

Psychiatry responds

The revisionist accounts, in themselves, can be seen as part of the moves towards community care. The response has come from both medicine and the humanities. It is hardly surprising that medicine (Clare, 1976; Wing, 1978) has sought to challenge accounts of the development of psychiatry that emphasise the elements of social control inherent in the profession. It is, however, somewhat ironic that three of the most powerful denouncers of this aspect of the exercise of professional power are psychiatrists themselves – Ronnie Laing, Thomas Szasz and David Cooper. The 'medical defence' is based on the clear view that the main aim of medicine is humanitarian and altruistic – that is, the relief of suffering. Within these accounts, there is an acceptance that certain practices would now be seen as cruel or even amount to torture. However, the argument is that this was the state of medical knowledge at the time. The intention was therapeutic within the medical definitions of the time. This is a key difference. Foucault does not see these interventions as therapeutic even within their historical context.

The critics of Foucault's work and other revisionist accounts have fallen into two very broad categories. The first focuses on what are seen as the fundamental historical flaws in the arguments. Sedgwick (1982) has demonstrated that the link Foucault makes between the decline in the treatment of leprosy and the development of psychiatric asylums does not hold. For Foucault, prior to the 'Great Confinement' the 'mad' had essentially been tolerated and allowed to live in society. At certain junctures, he argues that they had a status which enabled them to act as commentators on society. The role of the Fool in Shakespeare would be an example of this. Sedgwick argues that this portrayal of the mad as the lepers of modern society ignores the fact that they had been held in various forms of custody prior to the period Foucault is discussing. Rothman (1971) highlights the fact that the institutions that are usually described as a response to the problems of urbanisation developed in the USA in an overwhelmingly agrarian society.

A second critical approach to Foucault's work is concerned with the nature of morality and humanity in this discourse. Rothman (1971) argues that though Foucault's main thesis is conceptually attractive, it has imposed its own schema on a very complex story. He suggests that it is simply not possible to reduce the complex causes of the development of asylums to 'conspiratorial class strategies of divide and rule'. The founders of such institutions often came from religious backgrounds – for example, the Tukes of York – which would appear to be in conflict with their ascribed role as the oppressors of the wretched of the Earth. Ignatieff (1985) argues that the revisionist account falls down because of a series of misconceptions about the nature of society and social order. He suggests that accounts which assume that the State holds a monopoly of power over social control simplify the complex ways in which laws, morality and public sanctions combine. A further paradoxical feature is that some professions which become associated with the maintenance of social order appear on the surface to be committed to the relief of suffering. The revisionist account is based on a premise that social order is maintained by a combination of moral authority and practical power.

The revisionist accounts of the rise of asylums are very challenging as they force the reader to consider what we mean by such terms as progress and humane treatment. In addition, though this is not always made explicit, there is a consideration of the history of the institution from the viewpoint of the incarcerated. This is instinctively more appealing than the narrative which sees the history of the asylums as the struggle of psychiatrists to humanise an inhumane system. However, there is a fundamental difficulty with the revisionist accounts in that they appear only to be able to consider or describe human relations in the language of subordination and domination. In challenging the notion of progress, there seems to be a denial of its possible existence whatsoever. For Foucault, the development of the 'surveillance' state seems to lead him to conclude that the modernist attack on the customs, tradition and dogma of the *ancien regime* does not lead to the end of surveillance. There are new forms or technologies for power. For Stone (1982), this has had a destructive impact on the development of mental health services and the push towards deinstitutionalisation. He suggests that the attacks on institutional care led to a collapse in the belief in care itself.

The crisis in asylums

Giddens (1991) argues that modernity is characterised by the scope and nature of change along with the emergence of new institutional forms. One of the core beliefs of modernity is that rationality can be applied to the solution to social problems. Modernity brings with it a series of risks. The pre-modern or pre-industrial community was broken down by the development of an industrial market economy, which lacks the traditional patterns of authority and deference. This can be seen as liberating as it allows for the development of individualism. However, it is also accompanied by a sense of ambiguity. For example, the modern city can be seen as offering the opportunity for individual self-expression or as a shifting amoral and alienating wasteland. In such an environment, social order and control will become more problematic. The older systems were based on individual, family, kinship and hierarchical ties. Modernity requires a shift to a Weberian bureaucratic approach.

Psychiatry finds itself in an unusual position in modern medicine in that treatment can be imposed against the will of the patient. This group of thinkers (ie Laing, Szasz and Cooper) was concerned to develop a form of psychiatry that would adopt a much more holistic approach, which looked at the social causes of the distress that their patients were suffering. This would necessarily involve a paradigm shift from the institutional, coercive, pharmacological care that dominated at that time to voluntary, more psycho-dynamic, social and community-based models of service

The rates of admission to asylums had begun to decline in the 1930s. However, in 1954 there were still 154,000 patients in British mental hospitals. The criticisms of these institutions grew in the following decade. Barton (1959) identified the negative effects that institutionalisation could have on patients by comparing the behaviour of patients on long-stay wards to the observations of similar behaviour that he had observed among prisoners in concentration camps. Scott (1973) argued that the hospital itself made individuals passive. This meant that they would be unable to cope outside of the institution. This followed earlier work by Wing (1962), which had shown how the process of social withdrawal developed among long-stay patients. The majority of patients would fall into this category at this time. Overall, the picture was one of physically, socially and culturally isolated institutions cut off from the mainstream of health care and the wider society.

Goffman and total institutions

One of the most influential works in the literature of the crisis of the asylum is Goffman's *Asylums* (1961). Goffman's study of a large state psychiatric hospital has been seen as a pivotal point. He was concerned with the way that 'total institutions' function; in such institutions, he argued, there was a strict divide between staff and patients. The staff exercised control over all aspects of the patients' daily lives. The institution was so large, it could only function if it worked to a strict timetable, so the net result was that the organisational needs of the staff took precedence over any therapeutic needs of the individual patients. In this system, all aspects of daily living were monitored – if you were a patient, these aspects had to be carried out in front of staff. Two distinct and opposing cultures developed: that of the staff and patients. Goffman argued that patients need to maintain some sense of self, which they do by transgression or rule breaking – often in very minor ways. The staff then interpret these transgressions as evidence of illness or a lack of ability to stay within societal norms, thus justifying the original decision to admit the patient. This process ensures that the individual remains incarcerated. Rosenhan's (1975) famous pseudo-patient experiment emphasised that once someone has been diagnosed with a mental illness, there is a strong impulse to view all their behaviour through the prism of that diagnosis.

The nascent service user movements were influential in the migration from a system based on institutional care. In addition, the aims and aspirations of these groups chimed with other protest movements in society in the 1960s, such as the movement for civil rights, the feminist movement and gay rights. It should be noted that the history of psychiatry – and present-day practice – is scarred by its use to abuse women, members of ethnic minority communities and gay men and lesbians. The failings in hospital-based care were highlighted further by Martin (1985). Martin identified the ways in which these institutions had become isolated from mainstream service provision. As noted above, these institutions were geographically isolated from the communities that they served. Within the institutions, wards could become isolated with small numbers of staff in charge of very large numbers of patients. In his study, Martin also highlighted how, on the worst wards, there was a lack of leadership from consultant staff. The final factor that allowed for abuse was the isolation of the patients themselves. Martin found that patients with regular visitors were less likely to be abused. The overall picture is a very depressing one: large numbers of patients, little therapeutic work and poorly trained and poorly paid staff, which meant a lack of a sense of professionalism or a commitment to rehabilitation. If the hospital scandals that Martin studied were an impulse in the move towards community care, those policies in themselves have failed to prevent the repetition of such scandals – for example, Winterbourne View (see Special Edition: The Scandal of Winterbourne View Hospital (2013), *The Journal of Adult Protection* for a full discussion: www.emeraldinsight.com/toc/jap/15/4) – which have often identified patterns of abuse. The problems of the institution remain, even though the physical buildings have disappeared or been converted into designer flats.

The above is part of the liberal interpretation of the rise and fall of the asylums; it rests on the idea that the moves towards community care came about because of a humanitarian impulse to improve the quality of life for those suffering from long-term mental health problems. The most common explanation by policy makers for the decline of the asylums is the development of the new major tranquillisers. As Pilgrim and Rogers (2013) argue, this is a problematic explanation as it does not explain why community care came to be an umbrella policy or approach that was adopted across a range of settings, including groups such as people with learning disabilities, who were not actually treated with the medication that was alleged to be at the heart of the revolution. Another barrier that such an explanation would have to overcome would be the differential rates of the implementation of the policy of deinstitutionalisation.

The general portrayal of the asylum is one of a large dehumanising institution, which acted as a warehouse for the insane. In the literature, there have been relatively few attempts to look at the asylum as a functioning organism. Gittins (1998) wrote a study of one long-stay hospital, Severalls Hospital in Essex. The value of this study is that it acknowledges the complexity of such institutions and the motivations of the staff. The hospitals were communities and formed the focal point of the working lives of staff. Such institutions were usually the main employers in an area. It was not uncommon for members or generations of the same family to work at the same place. In addition, it is often possible to overlook the fact that, despite its many failings, the asylum was home for patients. As Gittins argues, for certain groups the asylum did fulfil its real role:

> *It seems that for some, particularly women, the fact that they could withdraw from the outside world, from family time and body time dominated by endless pregnancies, poverty and abuse, meant that life in Severalls could provide a time of peace and a possibility of asylum, in the original sense of the word.*
>
> (Gittins, 1998, p 9)

From a Marxist viewpoint, the genesis of the policy of the closure of long-stay institutions lies not in the laboratories of the major chemical companies, but in the offices of the treasuries of the governments involved. Scull (1977) argues that, following the post-war development of the Welfare State, the fiscal cost of maintaining asylums was too prohibitive. He argues that costs had risen in the US because workers had become more unionised, thus increasing wage rates, and the unpaid labour of patients was no longer used. For Scull, the consequences of this policy have been an unmitigated disaster for the mentally ill, who have been abandoned in 'deviant ghettoes'.

The politics of deinstitutionalisation

The origins of community care lay in an attempt to improve the care of one of the most marginalised groups in society. Whatever the original motives behind the establishment of the asylums, it was clear by the 1980s that they were no longer sustainable. This was not only on the grounds of the largely inadequate care that was provided but also, as was made explicit in the National Health Service and Community Care Act (1990), because the economic policies of the government of the time meant that new funding arrangements were demanded.

There is something of a false division between institutionalised and community care. The impulse behind community care was to improve the standards of mental health provision. Even in the most radical work, such as Laing, part of the recovery process involves a period in a therapeutic setting of one sort or another. The genus of community care is that prolonged periods of hospital care can in themselves be damaging and that services need to exist to intervene at an early stage to provide support to those suffering from any form of mental distress. This is a public health model of service provision that ideally develops tiers that will meet individual and community need. The asylum system resulted in a complete imbalance in that the services, such as they were, were almost all concentrated in this sector. The focus of modern mental health services is similarly unbalanced. The actuarial risk-dominated model of service provision focuses on smaller population groups. There is a danger that this means that the social determinants and the impact of mental illness become obscured or marginalised. This focus on audit, compliance and regulation has been termed 'bureau-medicalisation' (Webber, 2011).

The media portrayal of community care in the 1990s is virtually all based on cases of homicide or serious injury (Cummins, 2010; 2012). It is hardly surprising that the publications, which do much to contribute to the stigma that users of mental health services face, did not fully support a more progressive approach to service provision. The response has been a call for more coercive legislation, one which ultimately has been heeded by the current administration. However, the other element of the criticisms of deinstitutionalisation comes from those who one might suppose would support the principles of the policy, but feel that its introduction has not been adequately financed.

As Moon (2000) argues, there is a geographical paradox at the heart of the development of community care services. As several commentators note (Philo, 1997; Scull, 1989), the asylums were based on seclusion and concealment: the institutions served to cut off this group from the wider population. The experience of being a resident was potentially so damaging that you might never resume your former role. However, the move towards community care has not challenged this; in fact, as Wolff (2005) suggests, the institution has almost been reproduced in the community. Those with the most complex needs are often found living in the poorest neighbourhoods, in poor quality residential care homes, on the streets or, increasingly, in the prison system (Moon, 2000; Singleton et al, 1998). The overall picture is a very bleak one – so bleak in fact that the asylum system appears to have some advantages in that it was, at least, a community. For a variety of reasons – economic, social and political – the community has not proved up to the task of providing humane and effective services for those with the most complex needs.

Scull (1986) suggests that mental health services have been underfunded and not able to provide the continuity of care that the most vulnerable individuals in society need. These themes chime with the main conclusion of a series of inquiries into failures in community care services (Ritchie, 1994; Blom-Cooper et al, 1995). However, the response has been to focus on individuals or the legislative framework. Parton (1996) argues, in another context, that by focusing on dangerous individuals, one ignores dangerous conditions – thus not tackling the real source of the risk.

The thrust of mental health policy in the past 15 to 20 years can be viewed as a political response to the agenda created by a media focus on homicides and other serious events. A range of policies and legal changes – such as the Care Programme Approach (CPA), supervised discharge, supervision registers, *Modernising Mental Health Services* and national service frameworks – concentrated on essentially bureaucratic responses to the collapse of mental health services. This culminated in the reform of the MHA (1983) and the introduction of supervised community treatment orders (CTOs).

The justification for the development of community-based mental health services is based on moral and clinical arguments, and is a combination of idealistic and pragmatic approaches. The idealism can be seen in the human rights arguments that were put forward. Community-based services, it was argued, would be by definition more humane, although Lamb and Bachrach (2001) argue that this was based on a moral argument with little evidence to support it. Clearly, the supporters of community-based mental health services did not argue that asylums should be replaced by jails; however, deinstitutionalisation, a progressive policy aimed at reducing the civic and social isolation of the mentally ill, did not achieve its aims. Wolff (2005), Moon (2000) and Knowles (2000) show how asylums have been replaced by a fragmented and dislocated world of bedsits, housing projects, day centres or, increasingly, prisons and the CJS. This process of 'transinstitutionalisation' incorporates the ideas that individuals live in a community, but have little interaction with other citizens, and that major social interactions are with professionals paid to visit or, increasingly, monitor them. Other social outcomes such as physical health, which can be used as measures of citizenship or social inclusion, are also very poor indicators. Kelly (2005) uses the term 'structural violence', originally from liberation theology, to highlight the impact of a range of factors including health, mental health status and poverty, which impact on the mentally ill.

Community care as a 'moral panic'

The term 'community care' came to be used as shorthand for the reforms to health and social care introduced in the UK by the National Health Service and Community Care Act

(1990). This legislation was clearly driven in part by the Thatcherite agenda of reducing the welfare state and introducing elements of the market into service delivery (Gilmour, 1992). However, the reforms did place an emphasis on ensuring that institutional care was only used in circumstances when all community-based options had been exhausted. This aim was to be applied to the whole range of services for adults and children with health and social care needs, but the term soon became shorthand for community-based mental health services.

The reporting of and response to the policy of community care has many of the features of a 'moral panic'. Cohen (1972) is concerned with the ways in which the media, particularly the press and later TV, produced a series of stereotypical representations of events. Furedi (1994) has identified the ways in which newspapers continue to highlight new threats or potential threats to readers' health and well-being. Crime is a constant and very significant feature of the news. In Cohen's analysis, the moral panic begins with a period of concern about a social issue. These issues are very often related to youth culture and/or deviant subcultures. This process produces a 'folk devil'. In the reporting of mental health inquiries, the folk devil was clearly the 'schizophrenic', usually male, black and convicted of a crime of violence. Cross (2010) emphasises the continuing influence of representations of madness; these notions are transmitted through a range of popular cultural forms – song, film, TV drama and so on. Historically, physical representations of the 'mad' emphasise wild hair and physical size as signs of their irrationality and uncontrollability. It is interesting to note, in this context, the overlaps between these representations of the mad as almost bestial and deeply engrained racist stereotypes of black men. I have discussed these issues in relation to the racist media portrayal of Christopher Clunis (Cummins, 2010).

Hall et al (2013) seek to explore how and why particular themes, including crime and other deviant acts, produce such a reaction. He argues that social and moral issues are much more likely to be the source of these panics. There are certain areas, for example youth culture, drugs or lone parents, where there are recurring panics. Hall suggests that the panic is triggered by a particular event. He describes the ways in which these events cause 'public disquiet'. The response to this panic includes not only societal control mechanisms, such as the Courts, but also the media becomes an important mediating agency between the State and the formation of public opinion. In the case of mental health in the 1990s, key figures included Marjorie Wallace – journalist and founder of Schizophrenia a National Emergency (SANE) – and Jayne Zito, widow of Jonathan Zito and founder of the Zito Trust (Cummins, 2010). As Hall argues, such figures are seen as having expert knowledge and therefore play key roles in the development of public opinion.

The reporting of community care in the 1990s certainly had all the features of a moral panic (Butler and Drakeford, 2005). The crux of the media reporting was that there was a new threat from the 'mad' who had been released from asylums and posed an immediate violent threat to the local citizenry. The dynamic of the panic produced a call for 'something to be done'. In this case, the calls were not for the asylums to be rebuilt – this would have required a level of public investment that would not have been politically acceptable – but for new forms of surveillance and control.

Policy and legislative responses to the failings of community care

The response of successive UK governments since 1983 to the developing crisis in the provision of mental health services has been to focus on the legislative and policy framework. The main themes of these developments are moves to more systematic surveillance of patients and the audit of mental health professionals.

As the difficulties in mental health services increased, a series of measures were introduced. The circular *HC (90)23/LASSL(90)11* established the Care Programme Approach. The initial aim of the CPA was to develop a system of case management to ensure that services were provided to those in most need because of their mental health problems. It was a response to the failings of services highlighted by, for example, the Spokes Inquiry (DHSS, 1988) into the murder of social worker Isabel Schwartz, as well as wider concerns about the rise in homelessness. As Simpson et al (2003) argue, the aim of the CPA was initially to improve services. However, in its implementation, it shared a number of the wider characteristics of New Public Management, such as audit and regulation (Pollitt and Bouckaert, 2003). The establishment of the CPA brought with it added layers of bureaucracy and audit which did not seem to enhance the effective provision of mental health services. Each service user who was registered on the CPA was meant to have a care plan, key worker and regular reviews. The system became more focused on audit than the provision of care. As Simpson et al (2003) argue, there were few agreed procedures for risk assessments; care plans were often found to be ineffective and some areas had difficulty keeping up regular reviews. Service users and carers were more likely to be invited to reviews, but often found them formal and intimidating and arranged at the convenience of medical staff (p 493).

The introduction of the CPA was followed in 1993 by guidance on the introduction of supervision registers. People considered to be 'at risk of harming themselves or other people' could be placed on a supervision register, with the aim of ensuring that they remain in contact with mental health services. The argument here is not that these particular individuals did not need support from community-based mental health services; it is, rather, questioning not only the effectiveness of such measures as a means of enhancing the delivery of that support, but also noting the role that such developments play in the construction of the 'mad' stereotype.

Health Service Guidelines (94)/27 established that inquiries must take place following a homicide by a person with previous contact with mental health services. The Ritchie Inquiry (1994) into the care and treatment of Christopher Clunis made a series of recommendations, including the setting up of specialist teams to work with the mentally ill homeless. The Inquiry also recommended that consideration be given to the introduction of CTOs. If such legislation had existed then, no doubt Mr Clunis would have been made subject to its provisions. However, its possible efficacy in the turmoil of the inner-city mental health services of the time is highly questionable. The therapeutic state did not appear to have the resources to supervise Mr Clunis so it is not clear how this legislation would have changed that. In 1995 the Mental Health (Patients in the Community) Bill introduced 'supervised discharge', a short-lived piece of legislation which can be seen as a forerunner of the CTO legislation we have today. This was a rather confused piece of legislation. It attempted to impose conditions including contact with mental health professionals on the discharge of patients detained under section 3. These policy developments share some common themes. The focus is on the surveillance – in its widest sense – of discharged patients. There is an implicit assumption that these tragedies occurred because of patients failing to take medication. The service context of high levels of need and poorly organised and underfunded services is ignored. Ironically, such a description is finally provided in *Modernising Mental Health Services: Sound, Safe and Supportive* (Department of Health, 1998). This policy document was introduced by the then Secretary of State, Frank Dobson, with his famous observation that 'community care has failed'. Such policies not only add to the stigma that people with mental health problems face; they also inevitably deter individuals from seeking help.

Conclusion

In his highly influential analysis 'Governing through Crime', Jonathan Simon superbly dissects the ways in which debates around law and order have shifted. He also explores the ways those debates have come to have such a profound influence on the wider political culture. I have used this as a basis for an examination of the development of mental health policies in England and Wales (Cummins, 2012), in particular, the importance of high profile cases used as a call for new powers or legislation being a striking feature. Simon has highlighted that it has so far proved very difficult to challenge the terms on which these debates are conducted. In the mental health field, there was the introduction of increasingly restrictive and bureaucratic approaches focusing on the key areas of the audit culture – registration, review and inspection. In this schema, the actual quality of service provision is lost.

The response of successive governments since 1983 to the developing crisis in the provision of mental health services has been to focus on the legislative and policy framework. The WHO (2001) highlights that long-term facilities are still the most common form of service provision – 38% of countries worldwide have no community-based mental health services, whereas there has been a shift in service provision in North America and Europe towards this policy. At the same time, there has been a clear shift towards a more punitive prison policy.

Wacquant (2008; 2009a; 2009b) argues that throughout the industrialised world there have been large prison-building programmes and investment in their criminal justice systems. It should be noted that this process has been overseen by governments, particularly in the UK and USA, with a commitment to reducing both the role of the State and public spending. Gunn (2000) and Kelly (2007) found that the reduction in the number of psychiatric beds in the UK occurred at the same time as the rise in the prison population, as Lionel Penrose had predicted. The clash of the two policies outlined above – hospital closure and prison expansion – at first seems to provide evidence to support Penrose; they also create significant challenges for all those working in these fields. As Lord Bradley (2009) has highlighted, there is a need for all staff working in agencies in the CJS to receive training in relation to mental health issues.

Large and Nielssen (2009) undertook a review of Penrose's original hypothesis using data from 158 countries. They suggest one of the main features of Penrose's argument is that there is an unchanging proportion of any population that will need, or be deemed to need, some form of institutional control. They concluded that although there was a positive correlation between prison and psychiatric populations in low and middle income countries, there was no such relationship in high income countries. It is clear that in the UK, the prison population has risen significantly over the past 25 years. Wacquant (2009a) argues that prison policy has replaced welfare services as a means of responding to the needs of marginalised individuals and communities. Successive governments of differing political persuasions have been seemingly addicted to the expansion of the use of custody despite its well-documented failings to achieve its avowed aims. In addition, as Barr (2001) demonstrates, the 'zero tolerance' approach widely adopted in the privatising and policing of public space results in more mentally ill people being drawn into conflict with various public authorities.

Eastman and Starling (2006) observe that the treatment of the mentally ill was always a fundamental exploration of the balance between the rights and autonomy of the individual and a wider societal paternalism, as represented by professional decision makers. This debate arises because of the nature of mental illness and its impact on individuals. Only the extreme wings of libertarian thought (eg Szasz, 1963; 1971) do not accept the need for the therapeutic state to have powers to intervene when individuals are putting themselves or others at risk. There is a paradox at the heart of the development of mental health policy. In a number of ways, the rights of the mentally ill are on a much stronger footing than they have ever been. Those who experience discrimination as a result of their mental health problems have greater legal protections. In cases of compulsory detention, there is a new legal framework introduced to ensure compatibility with the provisions of the Human Rights Act (1998). In addition, there is wider public discussion and acknowledgement of the impact of mental illness; while the physical segregation in asylums has gone, stigma and fear remain. In addition, psychiatry, mental health social work, nursing and other disciplines have to offer a wider range of interventions to alleviate distress. However, the policies and legislation which will impact on those in greatest need do not reflect these progressive themes. The failure to provide a very vulnerable group – those suffering from severe mental illness who had been detained under section 3 MHA (1983) – with their legal entitlement to section 117 MHA aftercare was recast as a law and order issue. In doing so, a shift occurred in the balance between individuals and the State. It is a clear statement of the marginalised status of this group that this shift was hardly noticed by the wider community and there was certainly little effective opposition to it. The physical asylums may have gone but the CTOs may turn out to be the longest-lasting feature of their legacy.

Taking it further

Butler, I and Drakeford, M (2005) *Scandal, Social Work and Social Welfare*. Bristol: Policy Press.

Clare, A (1976) *Psychiatry in Dissent*. London: Tavistock.

Foucault, M (2001) *Madness and Civilisation* (translation Howard, R). New York: Vintage.

Goffman, E (1961) *Asylums: Essays on the Social Situation of Mental Patients and Other Inmates*. Harmondsworth: Penguin.

Gunn, J (2000) Future Directions for Treatment in Forensic Psychiatry. *British Journal of Psychiatry*, 176(4): 332–38.

Lamb, H L and Bachrach, L L (2001) Some Perspectives on Deinstitutionalization. *Psychiatric Services*, 52(8): 1039–45.

Moon, G (2000) Risk and Protection: The Discourse of Confinement in Contemporary Mental Health Policy. *Health & Place*, 6(3): 239–50.

Morriss, L (2014) Accomplishing Social Work Identity in Interprofessional Mental Health Teams Following the Implementation of the Mental Health Act 2007 (unpublished PhD thesis) [online]. Available at: usir.salford.ac.uk/30876/1/Thesis_final_version.pdf (accessed 15 December 2015).

Philo, C (1997) Across the Water: Reviewing Geographical Studies of Asylums and Other Mental Health Facilities. *Health & Place*, 3(2): 73–89.

Powell, E (1961) Enoch Powell's 1961 Speech [online]. Available at: www.canehill.org/history/enoch-powells-1961-speech (accessed 15 December 2015).

Rothman, D (1971) *The Discovery of the Asylum*. Boston: Little Brown & Company.

Szasz, T (1995) Idleness and Lawlessness in the Therapeutic State. *Society*, 32(4): 30–5.

Turner, T and Colombo, A (2008) Risk, in Tummey, R and Turner, T (eds), *Critical Issues in Mental Health*. Basingstoke: Palgrave Macmillan, 161–76.

Webber, M (2011) Social Work Needs More Research so It's Not Left Out in the Cold [online]. Available at: www.communitycare.co.uk/blogs/social-care-the-big-picture/2011/09/social-work-needs-more-research-so-its-not-left-out-in-the-cold/ (accessed 15 December 2015).

3 Madness and the Criminal Justice System: Ethical Issues

Critical questions

- *What role, if any, should mental illness play in decisions throughout the CJS?*

- *How useful is Nagel's concept of critical scrutiny?*

- *What is the significance of a move away from physical forms of punishment for the development of penal systems?*

- *What sentencing options do the Courts have if they wish to take account of an offender's mental health issues?*

- *Why is the term 'personality disorder' such a controversial one?*

This chapter will consider some of the ethical issues raised by the treatment of those with mental health problems who come into contact with the CJS. As we saw in the introduction, at every stage of the CJS there is the potential for the mental health status of an individual to be a factor in decision making.

The nature of the problem

The range of mental health needs and the great differences in patterns of offending make it difficult to make generalisations in this field. In addition, there are a number of ethical and philosophical issues that arise here relating to the diagnosis and treatment of mental illness (Eastman and Starling, 2006). Eastman and Starling note that a purely bio-medical model of illness cannot be applied in an easy fashion to mental illness. Mental illness has an impact on an individual's behaviour, thoughts and language. In a sense, it challenges our notions of personality and identity – the reason why we think people are ill is because they are 'not themselves' or 'behaving bizarrely' or because 'I have never seen him like this before'. The implications in the CJS field are also significant when questions of autonomy and responsibility are being considered. In addition, psychiatry and psychiatric diagnosis have a role to play in the CJS, which can lead to conflict; for example, the reform of the MHA (2007) has seen the creation of the term 'dangerous and severe personality disorder'. This term is, in effect, a legal categorisation cloaked in terms of psychiatric discourse.

Mental illness and the problem of autonomy

In the Anglo-American legal tradition, it is assumed that individuals are free to act or are autonomous. Autonomy in this context means that the individual is not coerced. Gross (1979) argues that for an individual to be held criminally liable they must have been in a position in which they could make a choice. As Lipkin (1990) argues, a person can only be regarded as responsible if their conduct is 'intentional, free and autonomous'. In following this model, it is important to examine the concept of autonomy as this will have particular implications for the legal treatment of offenders who are mentally disordered.

Nagel's concept of critical scrutiny

Nagel (1970) suggests that behaviour is intentional if the individual acts on a belief or desire. These must be independent and pass what he terms 'critical scrutiny'. An individual who is forced or coerced to take part in a criminal enterprise could argue that they were not responsible. This is not an uncommon argument, however the level of coercion has to be such that an individual has to be in immediate fear of their life for it to be successful. For example, contrast the case of a woman driving to work whose car is hijacked by bank robbers and who force her to drive them away, with the case of Patty Hearst (see www.britannica.com/biography/Patricia-Campbell-Hearst). In the first scenario, the woman would be seen as a victim rather than an offender. The case of Patty Hearst was clearly more complex, but in essence her defence was that she had been treated in such a fashion that she was no longer an autonomous individual.

The final leg of Nagel's schema is that the beliefs and desires that are the spring for action will pass critical scrutiny. The key here is the ability of the social self to examine the nature of beliefs and desires. This process would include the capacity to correct those beliefs or desires, which are flawed in some way or may lead to a course of action that could not be defended. Lipkin (1990) uses the examples of John Hinckley and Mark Chapman to demonstrate the application of this process and the implications for decisions of criminal responsibility. Hinckley's shooting of President Reagan was the result of a delusional belief system, in which not only did the President approve of his actions, but they would also lead to Jodie Foster becoming his lover. Both ideas were so bizarre that they could not pass any critical scrutiny. Mark Chapman has stated that his motivation for the murder of John Lennon was to promote the reading of *The Catcher in the Rye*. This is another example where the proffered explanation would not pass Nagel's test.

Morse (1999) discusses the issues of 'determinism or universal causation: partial causation; and free will or free choice'. These are clearly crucial in the development of the CJS and society's response to crime. For the Courts, responsibility is more than a decision about who committed an offence. Determinism seeks to argue that human behaviour can be explained in the same way that physical behaviour can – that there are laws of cause and effect. As Morse suggests, if one took this view to its logical conclusion, 'all behaviour would be excused and no one would be responsible'.

Punishment and moral responsibility

Such a totally mechanistic view would mean that our current practices of punishment would be highly morally dubious, as they would sanction the punishment of those who are not responsible for their actions – that is, all of us (Honderich, 2005). The argument for free will faces a mirror image of this problem, as it leads to the conclusion that as moral agents we are all responsible for our actions. In this schema, there would be no need for the Courts to consider the individual circumstances of a case. As noted above, this seems to run counter to strongly held cultural ideas surrounding the nature of individualism and what it means to be a person.

The law and the moral justification for punishment require that there is fault on the part of the offender, that they could have acted in some other way. The most commonly held view of punishment is a mixed model of just deserts combined with a consequentialist consideration of the outcomes of the imposition of punishment. Thus, an offender can only be punished if they deserve it because they have committed the offence and there is a positive outcome for society. This is usually justified by reducing offending by both that individual and the wider deterrent effect. From a purely retributive perspective, the desert component of the mixed model is sufficient. This would allow for individual punishment even if the net consequences for the wider society are negative. In both models, the desert requirement allows society to treat offenders as moral agents, who have chosen a particular course of action rather than being at the mercy of forces beyond their control.

There are two very important ways in which mental disorder may be vital in the consideration of the issue of criminal responsibility. The first relates to the formation of *mens rea.* Mental disorder may prevent the formation of the mental state, or it may help to establish a complete or partial excuse, thus affecting or limiting the range of punishments that the State may choose to exercise. A fundamental question is the extent, if any, to which mental disorder can be said to lead to the commission of an offence. The major argument in favour of the admission of a legal defence of insanity is that mental disorders affect the exercise of practical reason.

As Morse (1999) less than tactfully puts it, 'mental disorders affect practical reasoning primarily by producing crazy perceptions (hallucinations) and crazy beliefs (delusions) that give rise to grossly crazy reasons'. There is a further complication here in that the links between mental illness and offending are not as straightforward as this line of argument suggests. The Hinckley and Chapman cases are exceptions, in that the links between the delusional ideas and the criminal acts can be traced. This is not the case in a significant proportion of cases where involvement with the CJS is seen as a product of the failings of mental health systems (Wolff, 2005).

There are clearly major disputes about the nature of mental illness. However, leaving aside the issue of substance misuse and addiction, it is largely agreed that individuals are not responsible for the symptoms of mental illness and that such symptoms can affect the individual's ability to act as a moral agent. It is possible to identify moves against this position in the backlash against community care services for people with mental health problems. For example, the introduction of compulsory CTOs is, in part, based on the belief that community care tragedies such as the Clunis case (Ritchie, 1994) could have been avoided if patients had *not decided to refuse medication.* Part of the reason for the failure of Christopher Clunis's subsequent legal case was the view that his conviction indicated that he was responsible for his actions.

The extent to which mental disorder may affect an agent's ability to reason or apply critical scrutiny to a particular course of action is a variable that Courts will consider. Eastman and Starling (2006) strongly argue that mental illness is an issue for the CJS because of its effects on individual autonomy. It is a matter of degree that is altered not only by the nature and severity of the mental disorder, but also by other factors such as the efficacy of a particular course of treatment. It is important to note that mental disorder cannot be used to explain all offending. It can only be used to excuse, or be part of mitigation for, those offences where the disorder affected the reasoning that led to the commission of that crime.

There is an inherent danger that the portrayal of the effects of mental disorder is to turn those experiencing mental distress into machines. As well as being philosophically problematic, Morse (1999) suggests that such accounts are inaccurate. He argues that:

> *Even the most wildly delusional or hallucinating person retains the ability to act intentionally, to act for reasons. Actions that irrational perceptions and reasons motivate are nonetheless actions and are therefore distinguishable from involuntary bodily movements or from dissociated states that neurological disorders or extreme trauma, or the like, produce.*
>
> (Morse, 1999, p 162)

In all the examples referred to above, John Hinckley and Mark Chapman *both* had clear reasons for acting in the way they did. The issue for the CJS is to what extent the delusional basis of those reasons should be seen as a mitigating factor. In the case of Andrea Yates, the State of Texas initially sought to argue that no consideration at all should be given to these factors. The prosecution used aspects of Yates's behaviour – for example the fact that she dialled 911 – as evidence that she was not deluded but a callous killer (Denno, 2003).

Sentencing

The area where the issues of responsibility are given greatest prominence is sentencing. Mental disorder will be raised as a mitigating factor but it will also have an impact on the possible sentencing options open to the Courts. As noted above, punishment is inextricably linked to ideas of blameworthiness and responsibility. For example, children are treated differently in law – not because they are less responsible for an offence, but because they are not, by virtue of their age, deemed to be fully rational moral agents. There are those who oppose the notion of an insanity defence or the view that mental illness should be viewed as a mitigating factor. Chief among these is Szasz (1963; 1971). This is hardly surprising as he does not accept the commonly held notion of mental illness. It is suggested that if one accepts the arguments for an insanity defence then this opens the floodgates to a series of other 'defences' based on events that are outside of offenders' control – socio-economic status, genetic make-up or being a member of a minority group – which can be demonstrated to increase the likelihood that one will appear before the Courts.

Morse (1999) argues that such arguments rest on what he terms the 'fundamental psycho legal error ... confusing causation with excuse'. He argues that the issue should not be causation but rationality. The fact that someone is from a lower socio-economic background does not mean that they are irrational. It might be suggested that, in some cases, crime is a rational response to these circumstances. Such offenders can therefore be held responsible. In certain circumstances, mental disorder means that an offender is not rational and it would be unjust to punish such an individual.

Madness and punishment

Foucault: punishment and technologies of power

Foucault (1991) examined the development of systems of punishment in modern industrial societies. He suggested the English title *Discipline and Punish: The Birth of the Prison* for his major work in this area (*Surveiller et Punir*). In this, and in subsequent work, he examined the way in which modern systems of punishment have become more regularised. Foucault also outlines what he sees as a shift in the locus of punishment from the body to the mind of the offender.

Discipline and Punish opens with a description of the punishments inflicted on the attempted regicide Damiens. This grotesque event is outlined in great detail and Foucault owes a debt to Nietzsche here. Nietzsche (1996), in *On the Genealogy of Morals*, had concerned himself with the development of social mores. He saw this as a way in which man's elemental impulses are contained. In an approach, which finds echoes in Foucault's (1991, pp 60–1) description of the execution of Damiens, Nietzsche outlines the most gruesome of Old German punishments. These included stoning, boiling in oil or wine and smearing the transgressor with honey and leaving him to bake in the sun.

The most prominent feature of these punishments is their physical brutality; Nietzsche and Foucault do not approach such punishments as simply outbursts of savagery. Punishment is a regulated cultural practice. The physical nature of the punishment imposed on Damiens reflects the belief that crime was considered an offence against the monarch. This is not just the case for Damiens but for all offenders; the symbols and rituals of punishment reflect the value system of the society that produces it. In this process, Foucault notes that the offender is allowed to denounce the judges before the sentence is carried out. In this way, the established order is overturned for a moment before being restored and reinvigorated by the punishment.

Foucault (1991) contrasts the image of Damiens being pulled apart by horses – having been subjected to a litany of assaults, including having molten wax poured on him – with the sombre image of Foucher's prison timetable. For Foucault, this is a paradigmatic shift and the timetable represents the Enlightenment values of rationality. He argues that from the French Revolution onwards, punishment as a public spectacle declined. As the definition of what constituted a crime remained largely unchanged, this shift, Foucault argues, can only be explained by moves in societal values. For Foucault, this does not represent progress but, rather, a shift in the ways that social control and domination are exercised. These changes in the penal system – which are replicated, for Foucault, in education, psychiatry and the development of factory-based production – are attempts to develop efficiency. These themes are explored in more depth in his account of the life of *Pierre Rivière* (1992), who murdered members of his family. He uses this case to explore the battle between the legal and medical professions in this area, with both claiming the role of experts.

Foucault saw the period explored above as being the basis for what he termed the development of the modern technology of government. Centralised government became more powerful and had a greater regulatory role in the lives of the citizen. As noted above, this was not simply limited to 'outsiders' such as offenders or the mentally ill; for Foucault, Bentham's Panopticon was a metaphor for the ways in which bourgeois society regulated and controlled its citizens. Social developments in the organisation of education, work and punishment had created new systems of regulation, hence the symbolic importance and significance of Foucher's timetable. Such systems meant that there were better and more intrusive means of regulating individuals' activities, speech and sexuality.

Foucault and the body as a site of punishment

A major theme in Foucault's work is the way that society has moved from an emphasis on the exterior to the interior. These themes are explored in *Madness and Civilization* (2001) (see below). Foucault does not accept the traditional notion of progress in these areas. The changes in systems of punishment and the treatment of the mentally ill are not progressive, but are the application of what are seen as more efficient methods, and this reflects technological developments rather than a fundamental change in societal values. The wider function of punishment and the relationship between the individual and society remain unaltered.

For Foucault, the key feature of the penal or psychiatric system is the struggle of the individual against the wider societal impulses to conform or control. Thus, the changes in penal policy he discusses are the beginnings of new technologies of power, rather than elements of a humanitarian project to reform brutal regimes. As has been noted, for Foucault this change is, if anything, a regressive rather than a progressive step; punishments which require that offenders repent or change their attitudes lead to a greater control. In this line of argument, the sentence does not end until one becomes a respectable member of bourgeois society.

Madness and the Courts

The issues of autonomy, responsibility and the extent to which mental illness should be seen as a mitigating factor are played out in the Courts. In a number of cases, the issue is not whether an individual carried out an act, but whether their mental state means that they should not be regarded as culpable. The trial of Peter Sutcliffe, the so-called 'Yorkshire Ripper', is an example of this. In this case, his defence was not that he had not committed the offences: he entered a plea of guilty to manslaughter on the grounds of diminished responsibility. This was then rejected by the Crown. The trial then, in essence, became a debate about whether Sutcliffe was 'mad'. Sutcliffe was eventually found guilty and sentenced to life for the brutal murders of 13 women and seven further cases of attempted murder.

Sentencing under the Mental Health Act (1983)

The MHA (1983) gives the Courts powers to sentence offenders to be detained in psychiatric hospitals following convictions. It is a fundamental principle of mental health legislation that individuals can only be detained under its provisions if they are actually being treated for that mental disorder. This was established in the case of *Winterwerp v The Netherlands* (1979, 2 EHRR 387). The case established that unsound mind could not be accurately defined. However, for a detention to be valid it has to be based on objective medical evidence. The Court also held that the 'mental disorder' had to persist for the detention to continue to be valid.

It should be noted that the vast majority of offenders with mental health problems are not sentenced under these provisions. The powers are to be found under Part III of the MHA (1983). The most important differences between these and civil powers are that they follow on from conviction and form part of a criminal record. The decision to use these powers is a matter for the Courts acting on the expert opinion of psychiatrists and, occasionally, social workers. Courts have powers under sections 35, 36 and 38 to remand the accused for psychiatric assessment.

Mental health treatment requirement – community order

MHTR is available to the Courts as a sentencing option for community orders. These orders have rarely been used.

Section 37 hospital orders

The most common disposal following conviction is a section 37 hospital order. In theory, such an order could be made in any case where a sentence of imprisonment could be imposed and a mandatory sentence is not laid down in law. It could, therefore, not be imposed in a murder case as the mandatory sentence is life imprisonment. Section 37 has the same effect as a section 3 unless the Court imposes a restriction order under section 41.

Section 41 restriction orders

Following the use of section 37, the Crown Court has powers under section 41 of the MHA (1983) to impose a restriction order. This power is used on circumstances where the offender is deemed to pose a significant risk to the public. This group is often referred to as 'section 37/41 patients'. The net effect of such an order is that the patient cannot be discharged without the permission of the Home Secretary or a Mental Health Review Tribunal headed by a judge. This group of offenders has usually, but not exclusively, committed offences of serious violence, sexual assault, rape, manslaughter or arson. They do not constitute a homogeneous group but pose fundamental problems for service provision; for example, how do institutions manage the twin and often conflicting goals of punishment and therapy? It should also be noted that this group of patients is the subject of much media interest, not only because of the nature of the offences, but also the not uncommon belief that a mental health disposal indicates that they have escaped punishment.

The legal position of 'section 37/41 patients' is a complex balance of therapeutic aims within a framework which seeks to assure public protection. The provisions of section 37/41 can be used for offenders who meet the MHA (1983) definition of 'mentally disordered'. This would include patients suffering from major mental illnesses, or those with learning disabilities or regarded as having a personality disorder. The question of those patients who are personality disordered has been one that vexes policy makers. The Fallon Inquiry (1999) not only demonstrated the inadequacies of services, but also the tremendous challenges that this group of offenders poses for both criminal justice and mental health agencies.

Section 45A hybrid orders

The impact of such an order is essentially the same as section 37. However, under section 45A, once treatment is no longer necessary, the offender continues to serve out the remainder of their sentence in a prison.

A short history of personality disorder

The term 'personality disorder' is a controversial one in both psychiatry and the law. In fact, some would argue that the controversies over its use have rendered it almost meaningless. In 1997 the Fallon Inquiry was established to examine events and look at the management of Lawrence Ward (a specialist unit for patients suffering from personality disorders) at Ashworth Special Hospital. There are three special hospitals in England: Ashworth, Rampton and Broadmoor. These institutions are an uneasy mix of hospital and prison.

In theory, the individuals are patients and are therefore receiving treatment; however, all the patients are deemed to pose a very serious risk to the public. It is possible to be admitted to a special hospital without having committed any offence. This is not the case for the majority of patients, who have appeared in Court for the most serious of crimes, for example murder, manslaughter and sexual offences. The special hospital system has been the subject of a great deal of criticism and the Fallon Inquiry was the latest in a litany of official investigations into abuses of all kinds. The Inquiry investigated a series of allegations made by a patient called Stephen Doggett, who had absconded while on a period of escorted leave in Liverpool city centre. He went to Holland and forwarded a dossier to the hospital and his MP. The allegations were of an astonishing nature and included that drugs were being supplied to patients. The most serious allegation related to visits being made to Lawrence Ward by a young girl referred to as 'Girl A', who was visiting a man convicted of a series of horrendous sexual offences against children. The Fallon Inquiry had a wide remit to examine the running of Lawrence Ward, as well as the treatment of personality disordered offenders and individuals in the CJS and psychiatric systems.

The definition of personality disorder that was put to the Fallon Inquiry was as follows:

> *Personality disorders are currently defined as enduring patterns of cognition, affectivity, interpersonal behaviour, impulse that are culturally deviant, pervasive and inflexible and lead to distress or social impairment.*

(Fallon, 1999, p 307)

The above is not too far removed from Pinel's description of *manie sans délire* in 1801, in which 'specific features were absence of any appreciable alteration in the intellectual functions of perception, judgement, imagination but pronounced disorder of affective functions, blind impulse to acts of violence even murderous fury'.

Psychopathology

The terms 'psychopath' and 'psychopathology' were first coined by the German clinician Julius Ludwig August Koch and were first used to refer to all disorders of personality. However, they were subsequently modified by American psychiatrists and came to refer to those who demonstrated some form of anti-social behaviour. It was this usage that came to be adopted within British medicine.

The 1904 Royal Commission and the 1957 Percy Commission

The issue of how to respond to offenders who are considered to be mentally ill in some way – and therefore not viewed as responsible for their actions – has vexed policy makers for some considerable time. In 1904, the Royal Commission on the Care and Control of the Feeble-minded was established. One of its main concerns was to look at the position of those who were thought of as being 'mentally disordered' but who were not being certified under the existing Lunacy Acts. The Commission heard evidence that 'socially dangerous' people were not being certified because medical opinion held that insanity could not be diagnosed on conduct alone. The language used here is very interesting. The term 'socially dangerous' reflects the way that psychiatry was and, some would argue, is still used as a means of social control. The position that is being discussed is very similar to the current one: how does society respond to a group of offenders who are viewed as being in need of some form of treatment in addition to, or as an alternative to, punishment? The Commission proposed a new category of patient – the 'moral imbecile' – who, in addition to experiencing some form of mental illness, would exhibit 'strong vicious or criminal propensities on which punishment had little or no deterrent effect'. This concept was incorporated into the Mental Deficiency Act 1913. In 1957, the Percy Commission on the Law relating to Mental Illness and Mental Deficiency started its work. The Commission noted that the patients classified as 'mental defectives' by the 1913 Act were not a homogeneous group. The Commission felt that there was a need for a wider range of services and, in addition, argued that the existing legislation did not adequately address the position of how to deal with offenders of higher intelligence who came under the 1913 Act. Its solution was the creation of the category of 'psychopathic patient'. This development highlights the way that legal and medical definitions can diverge. The Percy Commission suggested that 'psychopathic' patients would include any type of aggressive or inadequate personality. However, at the time, the medical definition concentrated on emotional immaturity or instability when reaching such a diagnosis. The work of the Percy Commission resulted in the 1959 MHA, which defined 'psychopathic disorder' as a 'disorder or disability of mind, which results in abnormally aggressive or seriously irresponsible conduct'. It is also interesting to note that a 1959 Working Group on Special Hospitals concluded that psychopathic patients should be treated in separate units from mentally ill patients.

The 1975 Butler Committee

In 1975 the Butler Committee, which had been established to review the treatment of 'mentally abnormal offenders', argued that the term 'psychopathic disorder' should be removed from mental health legislation. It suggested that it should be replaced by the term 'personality disorder' as this would remove the confusion between the medical and legal uses of the term. The Butler Committee also recommended that a new form of indeterminate reviewable sentence should be introduced. The fundamental idea of this form of sentence was that the release of the patient/offender would be dependent on the perceived level of danger that this would entail.

The 1992 Reed Review

The final review that I wish to discuss took place in 1992. Dr John Reed chaired the *Review of Health and Social Services for Mentally Disordered Offenders and Others Requiring Similar Services*. The Reed Report recommended the creation of an extra 1500 medium-secure beds in smaller units than those in the special hospital system. Dr Reed commissioned a review that was carried out by Dr Bridget Dolan and Professor Jeremy Coid into the treatment of personality disorder. This review concluded that there was little research evidence of the effectiveness of various forms of treatment proposed for personality disorder. In his evidence to the Fallon Inquiry, Professor Blackburn argued that 'the legal category of psychopathic disorder bears little resemblance to the specific concept of psychopathic personality and does not denote a clinical entity'.

The legal, medical and philosophical issues that this creates were underlined by Coid (1992). In his research that was based on interviews at Broadmoor Special Hospital, he found that only 23% of male patients and 31% of female patients detained in the legal category of psychopathic disorder met the diagnostic criteria as outlined in Hare's (1996) *Psychopathy Checklist – Revised*. Coid's research is vital in this area because it illustrates the problems of definition. It is estimated that 10% of the general population suffer from some form of personality disorder. The medical definition is outlined in DSM-IV (American Psychiatric Association, 1994) and ICD-10 (WHO, 1992). Personality disorder can take many forms, including borderline, narcissistic, anti-social, compulsive and histrionic and, as Coid points out, it is possible for one individual to experience more than one form of the disorder. In addition, personality disorder does not exclude the existence of formal mental illnesses such as schizophrenia or manic depression. Coid found that 80% of the 'legal psychopaths' he interviewed met the clinical diagnosis for a mental illness as well.

There is a further problematic issue: the link, if any, between psychopathic disorder and offending. Baroness Wootton (1963) pointed out the circular nature of this argument. It might be suggested that the reason that someone commits an offence is that they are a psychopath; the evidence for this is that they have committed the offence. The relationship between personality disorder and violent or offending behaviour is much more complex and diffuse. Professor Blackburn, in his evidence to the Fallon Inquiry, suggested that a personality disorder may contribute to the development of a deviant lifestyle that results in some form of offending. In reality, there are so many factors that can lead to serious offending that it would be foolish to think that any diagnosis, let alone one as slippery as personality disorder, would offer a complete explanation of such events.

Reform of the Mental Health Act (2007)

In July 1999, the Home Office and Department of Health issued proposals concerned with the management of 'dangerous people with severe personality disorder'. The document was a joint publication because these individuals can be found in both the CJS and health system. The introduction to the document makes it clear that the vast majority of people with personality disorder cause distress to themselves and their families, but do not pose a risk to the wider community. The government argued that the proposals, which would only apply in England and Wales, would affect a group of about 2000 adults and suggested that 98% are men. At any one time the vast majority of these individuals are in prison or in a special hospital. If that is the case, one might ask why the government was so concerned about such a small group. The reply can be found in the introduction of this document:

> ... the law as it stands fails to protect the public from the danger these people represent because in many cases they have to be allowed to return to the community even though they remain dangerous.
>
> (Home Office and Department of Health, 1999)

Personality disorder and treatment

It is hardly surprising that given the doubts about the validity of the diagnosis of personality disorder, there are arguments about the efficacy or otherwise of treatment. At one end of the continuum of views is the idea that even if personality disorder does exist, it cannot be treated. It is clear that this view is held by a number of professionals. As Dr Chiswick pointed out in his evidence to the Fallon Inquiry, in 1995 thousands of violent offenders passed through the CJS, but only 12 were made subject to detention under section 37/41 and classified under the category of psychopathic disorder. The most common treatment approaches place an emphasis on psychological and social methods. Such techniques would include attempts to improve social skills and interpersonal functioning. Other themes would include looking at issues of victim awareness, anger management and sex education. All theories of the causality of personality disorder place an emphasis on childhood experiences, such as physical and sexual abuse. The treatment approaches are long-term, often painful, and require a massive investment in terms of resources; for example, it is suggested that it costs £38,000 per annum to keep a person with a personality disorder in a prison. The cost of detaining a similar individual in Broadmoor Special Hospital is estimated at £300,000 per annum.

Conclusion

Sentenced to psychiatry?

The issues of punishment and compulsory treatment can become confused; it would not be too surprising if those patients who are detained under the MHA do not see it as a form of punishment. Compulsory treatment carries many of the restrictions that one would normally associate with the features of punishment. There are clear restrictions in terms of liberty, access to information and visitors. It would be foolish to deny that it also carries with it social stigma that is an important feature of punishment. It has been suggested that criminal punishment is more transparent in that the offender, in the vast majority of cases, is given a final date on which they must be released. It might also be suggested that the criminal law makes it clear to the offender what is expected of them. Incentives are offered in terms of early release to encourage co-operative behaviour. The situation for those who have been diagnosed as being mentally ill is much less clear; all the models of punishment assume that the individual has been found guilty of an offence.

Responsibility

The issue of responsibility is linked to our notions of autonomy; in turn, defences of punishment and associated practices assume that individuals can be held responsible for their actions because they have exercised some degree of choice. In this area, it is clear that the law and the CJS operate in a world where the boundaries have become confused and blurred. As regards people who have been diagnosed as suffering from personality disorder, those lines become less distinct still. We have noted above that diagnosis and subsequent sentencing amount to a lottery. The CJS relies on a very clear-cut notion of responsibility, which in philosophical terms is committed to a notion of free will. If we choose to break the law, we can then be punished for our transgressions. The notion of personality disorder, as currently constituted in psychiatric terms, has within it a very real challenge to our ideas of responsibility; it goes further than traditional environmental explanations of criminal behaviour. However, the causal links between personality disorder and offending have not been adequately established. Of course, using the current definitions of personality disorder – which are very wide – this would be extremely difficult, if not impossible, to do.

The ethical issues that are raised force society to confront fundamental issues about the nature of personality, mental illness and appropriate treatment and punishment. This is particularly so in the case of the diagnosis and treatment of those who are regarded as being personality disordered. These issues – along with the fact that this group of offenders have often committed high profile offences, or those such as sadistic sexual murders which society finds most abhorrent – mean that the treatment of this group can obscure the wider issues.

Taking it further

American Psychiatric Association (1994) *DSM-IV-TR: Diagnostic and Statistical Manual of Mental Disorders*. Arlington, VA: American Psychiatric Press, Inc.

Burn, G (2004) *Somebody's Husband, Somebody's Son: The Story of the Yorkshire Ripper*. London: Faber and Faber.

Butler, Lord (1975) *Report of the Committee on Mentally Abnormal Offenders*. London: HMSO.

Coid, J (1992) DSM-III Diagnosis in Criminal Psychopaths: A Way Forward. *Criminal Behaviour and Mental Health*, 2(2): 78–94.

Denno, D W (2003) Who Is Andrea Yates? A Short Story About Insanity. *Duke Journal of Gender Law and Policy*, 10: 1–139.

Foucault, M (1991) *Discipline and Punish: The Birth of the Prison* (translation Sheridan, A). London: Penguin.

Foucault, M (1992) *I, Pierre Rivière, Having Slaughtered My Mother, My Sister, and My Brother: A Case of Parricide in the 19th Century*. Lincoln, NE: Bison Books.

Gross, H (1979) *A Theory of Criminal Justice*. Oxford: Oxford University Press.

Hare, R D (1996) *Psychopathy Checklist – Revised*. Toronto: Multi-Health Systems.

Home Office and Department of Health (1999) *Managing Dangerous Offenders with Severe Personality Disorder*. London: TSO.

Honderich, T (2005) *Punishment: The Supposed Justifications Revisited*. London: Pluto Press.

Morse, S J (1999) Craziness and Criminal Responsibility. *Behavioral Sciences & the Law*, 17(2): 147–64.

Nagel, T (1970) *The Possibility of Altruism*. Princeton, NJ: Princeton University Press.

Nye, R (2003) The Evolution of the Concept of Medicalisation in the Twentieth Century. *Journal of the History of Behavioural Sciences*, 39(2): 115–29.

Percy Commission (1957) *Report of the Royal Commission on the Law Relating to Mental Illness and Mental Deficiency 1954–1957* (Cmnd 169). London: HMSO.

Pinel, P (1801) *Traité Médico-philosophique sur l'Aliénation Mentale, où la Manie*. Paris: Richard, Caille et Ravier.

Reed, J (Chair) (1992) *Review of Health and Social Services for Mentally Disordered Offenders and Others Requiring Similar Services*. London: TSO.

WHO (1992) *The ICD-10 Classification of Mental and Behavioural Disorders: Clinical Descriptions and Diagnostic Guidelines*. Geneva: WHO.

Wootton, B (1963) *Crime and the Criminal Law*. London: Stevens & Sons.

4 Prison Mental Health and Forensic Services

The degree of civilisation in a society can be judged by entering its prisons.
Dostoyevsky, *The House of the Dead* (1862)

Critical questions

- *How do the general health care needs of offenders compare to the wider population?*

- *What are the barriers to the provision of mental health care in prisons?*

- *Why is the number of women in prison rising and what are the implications of this trend?*

- *What is the social work role within forensic mental health and secure settings?*

In this chapter, I will examine mental health issues that arise in prison settings. I will look at the needs of vulnerable groups as well as the difficulties of providing health care in custodial environments. The chapter then moves on to look at the provision of forensic mental health services in both hospital and community settings.

Health care in prisons

It is important to emphasise that it is not possible to look at the CJS as though it exists in some sort of splendid isolation from the wider society. Prisoners do not come from a representative cross-section of society – they are overwhelmingly young, male and poor. In the 1990s, the aim of government policy was to divert offenders with mental health problems from the CJS. This policy has not been successful; in fact, on the whole, prisoners have much higher health care (including mental health) needs than the general population. The Royal College of Nursing's guidance on nursing in the CJS notes that this is an area that requires highly developed skills and competencies, as the needs of prisoners are so complex. Butler et al (2004) note that there is a higher incidence of long-term and chronic conditions among the offender population compared to the general population. These areas include mental health issues, substance misuse, HIV, as well as diabetes and coronary heart disease. This reflects the fact that offenders come from poorer backgrounds and are much more likely to smoke and/or use drugs and alcohol. Chaotic lifestyles are not healthy and many offenders come from groups in the population – such as working class young men, IV drug users, sex workers and homeless people – who struggle to access standard health care services. In addition, the prison environment clearly has potential impacts on both areas of health – physical and mental. The current pressures on the prison system add to the difficulties in providing health care. High demands on staff and frequent moves of prisoners alongside other factors, such as the limited number of nursing and medical staff available, make continuity and consistency in care very difficult to achieve. There is one note of caution that needs to be exercised here: as Liebling (1994) observes, individual prisons are very different institutions. We need to look at not only the sort of prison – for example, Category A prisons will be very different from open ones – but also at the staff and organisational culture.

Women and prisons

Seddon (2007) suggests that there has long been a tendency to view all female criminality as evidence of mental illness. Women who commit crime clearly transgress in terms of offending, but they also violate patriarchal norms and expectations. It is important not to assume that all female prisoners are mentally ill but, nevertheless, the levels of psychological distress among this group are very high. Plugge et al (2008, p 631) conclude that 'women in custody are five times more likely to have a mental health concern than women in the general population, with 78% exhibiting some level of psychological disturbance when measured on reception to prison, compared with a figure of 15% for the general adult female population'. The physical health of women prisoners is also much lower than women in social class V – the group that experiences the poorest health. This is the broad general context for any analysis.

England and Wales have the highest female prison population in Western Europe. Women make up roughly 6% of the overall prison population. However, the rate of increase in the imprisonment of women has outstripped that of men. In the decade to 2005 – a period that saw the number of men in prison increase by 46% – the number of women in prison more than doubled. The Prison Reform Trust highlighted that in August 2012 there were 4132 women in prison (see www.prisonreformtrust.org.uk/Publications/Factfile). At roughly the same time in 1995, the figure was 1979 and in 2000, it was 3355. In August 2015, the Howard League for Penal Reform reported that there were 3932 women in prison, so there has been a slight drop since 2012 (see www.howardleague.org/weekly-prison-watch/).

BME women and prisons

The *Black Manifesto* (2010) highlighted the over-representation of women from BME communities in prison: 31% of the female prison population is from a BME background. There is also an increasing number of women in prison who are foreign nationals. In 2010, one in five women in prison was from this group – with Jamaican women being the largest number. These women are often from poor communities and have acted as couriers of drugs.

The Corston Inquiry (2007)

The Corston Inquiry was established following concerns about incidents of self-harm and suicide by women in prisons. Baroness Corston, in the foreword to the report, highlighted the fact that many women in prison have been sentenced to relatively short sentences – less than 12 months – for minor offences such as theft. This is not to deny that society should respond to such matters. The question to consider is whether the disruption that such a short sentence creates is justified. Women are much more likely to be sent to a prison that is further away from their community. We know that links with families and communities are one of the key factors in reintegration at the end of a prison sentence. The other very important area that needs to be taken into account here is the impact of imprisonment on families and children. This is true for all offenders but is particularly important in the case of women, who are much more likely to have the main or major childcaring responsibilities. Corston (2007) suggests that 'the effects on the 18,000 children every year whose mothers are sent to prison are so often nothing short of catastrophic' (p 1). The impact on children, combined with the high level of mental health needs among women in prison and the relatively minor nature of much of the offending that leads to their incarceration, has led to calls for more community-based sentences for this group. However, there is a smaller group of women who have committed much more serious offences where a custodial sentence is inevitable.

Mental health and women in prison

The Corston Inquiry paints a very frank portrait of the mental health needs of women in prison. As the Inquiry puts it:

> *These were the women I saw in prisons:*
>
> *Most were mothers. Some had their children with them immediately prior to custody, others had handed them to relatives or their children had been taken into care or adopted.*
>
> *Some were pregnant. Some discovered they were pregnant when they had no idea that that could be a possibility.*
>
> *They were drug users. It was not uncommon to have £200 a day crack and heroin habits disclosed.*
>
> *They were alcoholics.*
>
> *They often looked very thin and unwell.*
>
> *They had been sexually, emotionally and physically abused.*
>
> *They were not in control of their lives.*
>
> *They did not have many choices.*
>
> *They were noisy and at first sight confident and brash but this belied their frailty and vulnerability and masked their lack of self-confidence and esteem.*
>
> *They self harmed.*

They had mental health problems.

They were poor.

They were not all the same, they were individuals.

There were significant minority groups, including BME and foreign national women.

(Corston Inquiry, 2007, p 4)

The above is a reflection of the wider experiences that lead women into contact with the CJS in the first place. One in four women in prison had spent part of their childhood in care; nearly 40% had effectively left school before they were 16. Corston catalogues the extent and deeply engrained nature of the problems that women in prison face. As with all figures in this area, it is important to note that the risk factors are much more common in offender rather than in general populations. Even allowing for that, the levels of mental distress are, to my mind, both astonishing and deeply troubling. The following gives a brief snapshot:

37% had attempted suicide at some time in their life.

51% have severe and enduring mental illness.

47% a major depressive disorder.

6% psychosis.

3% schizophrenia.

50% + suffered domestic violence.

One in three women in prison have been subjected to sexual violence.

(Corston Inquiry, 2007)

A 2008 review by the Chief Inspectors of Prisons and Probation of those subject to indeterminate sentences for public protection found that over 80% of women on these orders had committed offences of arson (see www.justiceinspectorates.gov.uk/probation/wp-content/uploads/sites/5/2014/03/hmip_ipp_thematic-rps.pdf). Women prisoners themselves face particular difficulties; for example, they face disciplinary proceedings at higher rates than men. The Ministry of Justice suggests that this indicates that mental health issues mean it is often more difficult for women to adapt to prison regimes and to follow the rules (see www.gov.uk/government/uploads/system/uploads/attachment_data/file/220060/gender-substance-misuse-mental-health-prisoners.pdf).

Women, self-harm and suicide in prison

The Corston Inquiry was established following the deaths of six women at Styal Prison. The State has a clear moral and legal duty to ensure the safety of those that it has detained or imprisoned. Many of the social factors that are part of the reasons why women end up in prison – childhood sexual abuse, domestic violence, substance abuse and experiences of care or chaotic lifestyles – are also risk factors for suicide and self-harm. Comparisons between the rates of suicide among women in prison and the wider population therefore need to be approached with caution. Hawton et al's (2014) study of self-harm and suicide indicates that these are ongoing issues for women's prisons. Self-harm is a risk factor for suicide and an estimated 20–24% of women in prison self-harm. In 2014, women accounted for 26% of all incidents of self-harm in prisons, despite being only 5% of the overall population. The Chief Inspector of Prisons' most recent report highlights a drop in the number of self-inflicted deaths in women's prisons. In 2013–14 there was one, compared with three in the previous year. This is clearly a welcome trend.

Campaigning for reform

It is important to emphasise that the broad health care needs of prisoners are much higher than those of the general population. In addition, the prison environment has the potential to exacerbate mental health problems, and the organisation and delivery of health care in such settings face a number of barriers. The rise in the numbers of those in prison increases the difficulties in this area. The 2009 Bradley Report concluded that there are now more people with mental health problems in prison than ever before, and that 'while public protection remains the priority ... custody can exacerbate mental ill health, heighten vulnerability and increase the risk of self-harm and suicide' (p 1). There have been significant moves to improve the delivery of mental health care in prisons – for example, in the establishment of mental health inreach teams – but these developments are starting from a relatively low base. These moves are partly a response to campaigns by organisations such as the Prison Reform Trust, the Howard League for Penal Reform and other more local groups. The National Federation of Women's Institutes launched a 'Care Not Custody' campaign and in June 2008 its Annual General Meeting passed, by an overwhelming majority, the following mandate:

> In view of the adverse effect on families of the imprisonment of people with severe mental health problems, this resolution urges HM Government to provide treatment and therapy in a more appropriate and secure residential environment.
> (www.thewi.org.uk/campaigns/current-campaigns-and-initiatives/care-not-custody/campaign-overview)

The experience of imprisonment

The Chief Inspector of Prisons, as well as inspecting individual prisons, produces an annual report – with echoes here of John Howard's (1780) *The State of the Prisons in England and Wales*. In the 1980s and 1990s, Chief Inspectors such as Sir Stephen Tumin and Lord David Ramsbotham became high profile media figures, regularly appearing on TV and radio to discuss their latest – usually highly critical – reports. There is an irony that the strongest criticism of penal policy came from these two Oxbridge-educated establishment figures. Sir Stephen was a High Court Judge and Lord Ramsbotham a General. The current Chief Inspector, Nick Hardwick, has been similarly critical of prison regimes and has not had his contract renewed as a result. The Inspectorate has developed the concept of the 'healthy prison' and inspects prisons accordingly. This is a values-based approach and is, in itself, a radical departure from the managerialism that so blights other inspection regimes. The key areas that are examined are as follows:

- Safety – Prisoners, particularly the most vulnerable, are held safely.

- Respect – Prisoners are treated with respect for their human dignity.

- Purposeful activity – Prisoners are able, and expected, to engage in activity that is likely to benefit them.

- Resettlement – Prisoners are prepared for their release into the community and helped to reduce the likelihood of re-offending.

> (www.justiceinspectorates.gov.uk/hmiprisons/wp-content/uploads/
> sites/4/2015/07/HMIP-AR_2014-15_TSO_Final1.pdf)

All of the above have the potential for a positive impact on the mental health of individuals.

One of the main concerns of this book is the way in which the expansion of the use of imprisonment has occurred with very little opposition or interest from social work. In addition, the profession and academia have largely overlooked the deteriorating conditions in prisons. The CJS, once a key area of concern for social work as a profession, seems to have almost disappeared from wider debates in the field. These are now dominated by child protection. I am obviously not suggesting that these issues are not important – they clearly are – however, the links between the CJS and such areas need to be considered and emphasised. As we noted above, the imprisonment of women also has impacts on the development and life prospects of their children. We need to examine the care–prison pipeline and take more actions to break it. Far too often, policy makers and the media ignore the fact that those in the CJS are either children or those who have been subjected to damaging and abusive experiences as children. The experience of imprisonment often does little to acknowledge this or attempt to deal with these longstanding issues.

Male prisons

Mental health in male prisons

Singleton et al's (1998) research remains the leading study in this field. The study interviewed over 64,000 prisoners in more than 130 penal institutions. Only one in ten prisoners did not show any signs of mental disorder. In addition, alcohol and drug misuse were very common. These figures are nearly 20 years old so need to be treated with caution; however, they give a clear picture of the position at that time. The prison population has virtually doubled in the period since – yet the issues of mental health and substance misuse remain. The Mental Health Foundation summarised the key findings:

- *A high proportion of both remand and sentenced prisoners were found to have two or more types of 'mental disorder'.*

- *Sleep problems, general worry (excluding concerns about physical health), fatigue and depression were prevalent among all prisoners, especially those on remand.*

- *55% of prisoners had some form of 'neurotic disorder'. Neurotic disorder was found in 59% of men on remand and 40% of sentenced men compared with 76% of women on remand and 63% of sentenced women.*

- *10% of prisoners displayed symptoms of functional psychosis (the figure for the general population is 0.4%). This constituted 7% of male sentenced, 10% of male remand, and 14% of female prisoners. Schizophrenia or delusional problems were the most prevalent.*

- *65% had some form of 'personality disorder': 78% of male remand, 64% of male sentenced, and 50% of female prisoners (remand and sentenced). The most common form was antisocial personality disorder.*

- *Reported suicidal thoughts were very high: 46% of male remand prisoners had thought about suicide in their lifetime, 35% in the last year, and 12% in the week prior to interview. The rate for females on remand was even higher.*

- *27% of male remand prisoners had attempted suicide at some point in their life: 15% in the last year, and 2% in the week before the interview. The high level of past suicide attempts suggests that suicide is not necessarily a result of the prison situation alone.*

- *More than half of male prisoners (58% of male remand and 63% of male sentenced) had misused alcohol to a significant extent, compared with 36% of female remand prisoners and 39% of female sentenced prisoners.*

- *There was little difference in drug dependence between men and women, although women were more likely than men to be dependent on heroin and non-prescribed methadone.*

(www.mentalhealthfoundation.org.uk)

The prison environment can be viewed as a perfect paradigm of Julian Tudor Hart's (1971) inverse care law – those with the greatest health care needs have the least access to services.

Suicide in male prisons

The WHO (2007) reported that suicide is the most common cause of death in prisons. Fazel et al (2009) indicate that the prison rate is between three and six times that of community settings. This reflects the higher incidence of risk factors among prison populations. In the decade to 2014, a series of measures was introduced to improve the assessment of those prisoners at risk of self-harm and suicide. These measures led to a reduction in the rate of suicide – from 140 per 100,000 in 1999 to 70 per 100,000 in 2012 (Ministry of Justice, 2015). However, this very welcome downward turn was reversed to 100 per 100,000 in 2014.

As well as pre-existing health needs, offenders are also at risk of health problems created as a consequence of imprisonment. The identified risk factors for suicide, such as substance misuse, a history of mental illness and unemployment, are much more prevalent in offenders than the wider population. These factors, and the difficulties they cause, are demonstrated very clearly in Rivlin et al's (2010) study of psychiatric disorders among male prisoners who had attempted suicide. The authors interviewed 60 prisoners who had made near-lethal attempts on their own lives, and compared their experiences with those of a control group of 60 other prisoners. The most common methods used were hanging or ligatures (40), followed by serious incidents of cutting (12). Institutions such as prisons or psychiatric units try to design out or reduce the opportunities for self-harm and injury – but it is clearly not possible to do this completely: 59 of the incidents took place in the prisoners' own cells.

The study demonstrated that prisoners who had no educational qualifications, who had been in prison previously, who had been imprisoned for less than 30 days, or who had been in their current prison for less than 30 days were much more likely to attempt suicide than other prisoners. The research also emphasises one of the problems with trying to tackle this issue: in a population where self-harm, suicide attempts and mental health problems are relatively common, identifying those most likely to take their own lives can be difficult. Nevertheless, the finding that only 24 (40%) of the cases were identified as being 'at risk' for suicide at the time of their attempt indicates that there is scope for improving detection of those at risk of suicide, perhaps with a structured suicide screening tool. The study suggests that such an instrument should include questions regarding prisoners' history of psychiatric contact, previous self-harming and suicidal behaviour (especially if this occurred while in prison) and current psychiatric disorders.

As Rivlin et al's work shows, many suicidal prisoners are serving short sentences; all the research shows that short sentences serve no real purpose and do more harm than good. This is not an argument for longer sentences, but rather for community-based alternatives that tackle the causes of offending – be they alcohol, drug misuse or a lack of training or skills. Until society tackles its own addiction to imprisonment, prison staff will still struggle to safeguard their most vulnerable prisoners.

Older prisoners

The general assumption is that prisoners are young men. As Age UK notes, about 8,000 or almost one in ten prisoners are over 50 years of age (see www.ageuk.org.uk/documents/en-gb/for-professionals/government-and-society/older%20prisoners%20guide_pro.pdf?dtrk=true). The overwhelming majority are male with an estimated 350 women in prison. The poor physical health status of prisoners has to be taken into account here. Older prisoners are the fastest growing section of the prison population. A number are serving longer sentences for serious crimes – it is estimated that around 40% of this group are serving sentences for sexual offences. There are of course a number of high profile examples, such as Stuart Hall and Rolf Harris, who have been convicted of historical sexual offences in their 80s. In 2014, the Prison Reform Trust highlighted that there were 102 people in prison aged 80 and over; five people in prison were 90 or older. One has to question what risks this group of prisoners actually poses to the wider society.

Prisons and prison regimes are designed for able-bodied young men. The wider problems of ageing, of course, apply to older prisoners but will be exacerbated by prison regimes. The sorts of difficulties that prisoners may face are illustrated by the Prison Reform Trust:

I am 65 years old and work full time … Really I am one of the lucky ones. Some of the prisoners are disabled 70, 80 years old, locked behind their doors, no TVs, some have no radio, banged up 5.30 evening until 10, 11 am next day with no hot water, not opening for hot water for a drink. Not opening for them to go for medication, resulting in one man being taken to hospital. Another has self harmed.
(www.prisonreformtrust.org.uk/PressPolicy/News/vw/1/ItemID/245)

The introduction of the Care Act (2014) will impose a duty on local authorities and prison staff to meet the social care needs of those who have been sentenced by the Courts. In terms of mental health issues, an older population means that there will be more prisoners who will develop dementia and other related illnesses. The CJS has a number of challenges to face in this area in trying to meet the needs of older prisoners. This will include the wider provision of specialist physical and mental health services for older prisoners, but also much broader questions such as whether there should be, as in other countries, an age above which offenders cannot be imprisoned.

Forensic mental health services

As the Singleton et al (1998) study indicates, about 90% of prisoners can be viewed as having a mental health problem. Forensic services exist for those who have come into contact with the CJS and have a mental illness. These interventions, as this book demonstrates, can come at any point of the process. There are three levels, high medium and low, and three high-secure institutions (special hospitals) in England – Rampton, Broadmoor and Ashworth – and 800 high-secure beds These institutions are an uneasy mix of hospital and prison. In theory, the individuals are patients and therefore receiving treatment. However, all the patients are deemed to pose a very serious risk to the public. It is possible to be admitted to a special hospital without having committed any offence. This is not the case for the majority of patients, who have appeared in Court for the most serious of crimes. There are, of course, several high profile patients in these hospitals and the media continues to try and obtain information about such patients. The patients are detained under the MHA 1983 under conditions of high security because they 'pose a grave and immediate danger to the public'. There are around 3500 medium-secure beds and 35% of these are provided by private providers.

As with the prison population, the number of people detained in forensic settings has been increasing. The majority of this increase has been in medium-secure settings. In a number of ways, the special hospitals appear remote from the wider mental health system; however, it is important to recognise that most patients are transferred to medium-secure units for further treatment and are eventually discharged into the community under supervision. The *Count Me In Census* (Healthcare Commission, 2007) indicated that 55% were under the age of 40. Approximately 12% of this cohort is female – more than double the total of women in the prison population. The 2007 figures show that 76% of patients were diagnosed with a mental illness and 12% with a psychopathic disorder.

Admission to forensic services and length of stay

Patients can be admitted to forensic services directly from prison, on sentences by the Courts or directly from community services. Patients who have been discharged can also be recalled to secure provision if there are concerns that their mental health has deteriorated. In 2006, 64% of admissions (n=961) were from prison transfers, either after sentencing or while the patient was on remand; 20% (293) were patients who were sentenced under the provisions of section 37/41. There were 197 recalls after conditional discharge and 45 patients who were admitted because they were deemed unfit to plead (not guilty by reason of insanity). There have been concerns about transfer waiting times from prison: in 2006, an average of 42 prisoners per quarter waited more than three months for a move to forensic psychiatric provision. The most common reason was a lack of beds (see www.gov.uk/government/uploads/system/uploads/attachment_data/file/218001/mentally-disordered-offenders-2008.pdf).

The image of forensic services, particularly special hospitals, is that patients will never be discharged. This is probably the result of the media focus on high profile patients, some of whom have been sentenced to whole-life terms of imprisonment. The above official government statistics, published in 2008, indicate that more than 50% of patients were discharged from forensic services in under five years. In fact, 34% had an admission of under two years. In this survey, 20% of patients had been admitted for between five and ten years; 9% (at that time a total of 283 patients) had been in forensic services for over 20 years – 83 (3% of the total population) had been in the services for over 30 years. It is perhaps not that surprising that, of those diagnosed with 'psychopathic disorder', 50% had spent more than ten years in hospital.

Tables 4.1, 4.2 and 4.3 show trends in admission to forensic services over the decade 1998–2008.

Table 4.1 Admissions to forensic services by gender

Year	1998	1999	2000	2001	2002	2003	2004	2005	2006	2007	2008
Male	2430	2515	2536	2636	2631	2720	2886	2984	3159	3448	3460
Female	319	327	322	333	358	398	396	411	442	458	477
All patients	2749	2842	2858	2969	2989	3118	3282	3395	3601	3906	3937

Table 4.2 Hospital admissions

Type of hospital	Gender	1998	1999	2000	2001	2002	2003	2004	2005	2006	2007	2008
High security hospital	Male	105	98	80	78	71	90	123	104	107	81	109
	Female	12	19	14	10	6	11	7	8	4	3	1
	All patients	117	117	94	88	77	101	130	112	111	84	110
Other hospital	Male	871	909	800	821	823	858	1095	1109	1172	1215	1212
	Female	103	93	78	88	106	127	104	129	157	159	179
	All patients	974	1002	878	909	929	985	1199	1238	1329	1374	1391
All hospitals	Male	976	1007	880	899	894	948	1218	1213	1279	1296	1321
	Female	115	112	92	98	112	138	111	137	161	162	180
	All patients	1091	1119	972	997	1006	1086	1329	1350	1440	1458	1501

Table **4.3** Legal status of patients

Legal category	1998	1999	2000	2001	2002	2003	2004	2005	2006	2007	2008
Transferred from prison service establishment after sentence	402	385	386	402	410	489	505	561	627	684	703
Transferred from prison service establishment while unsentenced or untried	168	151	151	160	141	174	189	218	175	284	234
All transferred from prison	570	536	537	562	551	663	694	779	802	968	937
Hospital order with restriction order	1758	1852	1860	1910	1939	1909	1978	2344	2492	2624	2678
Recalled after conditional discharge	266	287	285	287	270	308	351	–	–	–	–
Transferred from Scotland, Northern Ireland, etc.	3	3	3	3	3	3	3	2	3	8	7
Unfit to plead	110	120	124	152	170	180	205	212	234	244	255
Not guilty by reason of insanity	25	23	28	34	39	37	35	42	51	46	47
Hospital and limitation direction	–	5	7	10	9	11	10	11	14	16	13
Other	17	16	14	11	8	7	6	5	5	0	0
All legal categories	2749	2842	2858	2969	2989	3118	3282	3395	3601	3906	3937

Forensic mental health social work

As was noted earlier, there is no clearly agreed definition of a 'mentally disordered offender'; the term covers a very broad group of people. It is a moot point as to whether there is a distinct area of mental health social work practice that could be seen as 'forensic' work. The basic values and principles in this area are, to my mind, no different from those that apply across the wider discipline. The picture is clouded by the issues of risk alongside the legal basis for practice. The term has come to be a shorthand for social workers who work with those in secure mental health services, rather than with any individual with a mental health problem who appears before the Courts, or is in contact with the CJS. In this section, I will be examining the roles that social workers take on across the forensic setting.

Social work in secure settings

Social workers in secure settings are involved in the provision of the full range of social work services to patients, families and carers. The fact that the environment is a secure one adds to the pressures that they face and may create a particular range of challenges. It does not change the fundamental role, which is to ensure that the social care needs of service users are addressed and that their views, alongside those of their families, are taken into account when decisions about treatment and rehabilitation are taken. Patients are not detained under section 37/41 unless there are very serious concerns about the risk that they pose to the wider community. Therefore, risk assessment is a key area of concern, particularly when decisions about discharge or moving from a high- to a medium-secure environment are being considered. Social workers will be involved in documenting a full social history of the service user so as to ensure that this is the most appropriate environment. Social workers will have particular skills and knowledge in this area, as part of any risk assessment is to consider much broader concerns – such as the views of victims, any child protection or adult safeguarding issues, views of family members and community responses to the original offence. Social workers will be involved with supporting family members who are coming to terms with not only the fact that their loved one has a mental illness, but also that they have committed a very serious offence. Like all systems – to outsiders or those with little experience of them – forensic services can be a maze, so families often need very practical advice on matters, such as visiting, as well as an explanation of the jargon that professionals use. Patients who are detained under section 37/41 are entitled to appeal to a tribunal. As with all tribunals, a social circumstance report is required, which will be prepared by a social worker. This group of patients are entitled to section 117 MHA aftercare and social workers will be involved in the drawing up of these plans – for example, making referrals to appropriate accommodation and liaising with local mental health services.

Social supervision

Section 42 MHA allows for the Secretary of State to discharge a restricted patient; this is a conditional discharge, as the patient remains subject to recall at any time. A first tribunal has a similar power to conditionally discharge a restricted patient. The Ministry of Justice's (2009) guidance on social supervision indicates that in this group of patients, 'over 50%

have been convicted of offences of violence against the person, a further 12% convicted of sexual offences and 12% of arson'. The management of this group, therefore, inevitably focuses on risk and risk management.

There are about 1500 conditionally discharged patients subject to what is termed 'social supervision'. The requirements of supervision vary, depending not only on the mental health and social care needs of the individual, but also on the nature of the offence committed. The conditions that are attached to the discharge of such patients will include residence, continuation of treatment and regular contact with the professionals involved. The social supervisor should normally be a social worker who is an AMHP or a probation officer. These are complex and demanding cases, which require experienced and confident professionals. The relationship with a social supervisor is rather different from the usual social worker/service user one, and there is debate as to whether 'service user' is an appropriate term here. In essence, the patient has to consult with, and gain, the social supervisor's approval for any significant change in their circumstances; this would include decisions not only about where they live and work, but also on financial and personal matters. The social supervisor, along with the psychiatrist and other members of the team, will have very detailed information about the individual's mental health and offending history. There may be occasions where the decision is taken – in the interests of the patient, other individuals or the wider community – for information to be disclosed that would not be normally.

The management of this group of patients is undertaken by staff in the Mental Health Casework unit in the Ministry of Justice. The social supervisor has to provide regular detailed updates to the Ministry of Justice on the progress of the individual under supervision. It is important that these reports provide a complete picture of the case. As the Ministry of Justice notes, one of the themes in reports into homicides committed by conditionally discharged patients is a professional reluctance for supervisors to report negative behaviours or concerns. Social work in this setting can thus be seen as a challenge to some of the traditional approaches of the wider profession.

Multi-agency public protection arrangements

The MAPPA system was introduced by the Criminal Justice and Courts Services Act 2000. MAPPA panels bring together staff from a range of agencies, including the police, probation and relevant mental health services to assess and manage those offenders viewed as posing the greatest risk to the wider community. Other agencies may be involved in MAPPA, depending on the individual circumstances of the case and the nature of the potential risk that the offender is seen to pose. Not all mentally disordered offenders will come within the remit of MAPPA.

Which offenders are subject to MAPPA?

There are three categories of offenders that are managed by the MAPPA system (Ministry of Justice, 2009):

- All registered sex offenders – Violent and Sex Offender Register (ViSOR) is a database of offenders registered with the local police under the terms of the Sexual

Offences Act 2003. There are a series of time periods for registration – for those on a restriction order, they must be on the register for life.

* Offenders who have been sentenced to a period of 12 months or more in prison for a sexual or violent offence.

* A convicted offender who is regarded as posing a 'risk of serious harm to the public'.

MAPPA and levels of risk

MAPPA panels must first ensure that they have identified the offenders living in their area who meet the above criteria. A risk assessment is then completed. Agencies are allowed to share confidential information in the management of this group of offenders. MAPPA panels identify three levels:

* Level 1: normal inter-agency management arrangements are seen as sufficient to manage the risks.

* Level 2: Multi-agency public protection meetings will be held regularly to discuss the risk management arrangements that are in place.

* Level 3: The level of risks is such that senior managers attend the multi-agency public protection meetings to ensure that the risk management plans are appropriate, and also that resources are in place to implement them.

It is likely that the nature of the offences and the risk of further offending mean that discharged restricted patients will be considered as level 3 cases. In addition, MAPPA has to consider the responses of individuals and the wider community to high profile cases – for example, the potential for public disorder if an offender returns to an area. The risk management plans will include considerations such as accommodation and the sorts of conditions that need to be imposed – for example, an offender might be excluded from an area or from contact with a particular individual. Social workers will have an input into this system at both an individual and organisational level.

Taking it further

Bradley, K (2009) *The Bradley Report: Lord Bradley's Review of People with Mental Health Problems or Learning Disabilities in the Criminal Justice System*. London: Department of Health.

Butler, T, Karaminia, A, Levy, M and Murphy, M (2004) The Self-reported Health Status of Prisoners in New South Wales. *Australian and New Zealand Journal of Public Health*, 28(4): 344–50.

Corston, J (Chair) (2007) A Report by Baroness Jean Corston of a Review of Women with Particular Vulnerabilities in the Criminal Justice System [online]. Available at: www.justice.gov.uk/publications/docs/corston-report-march-2007.pdf (accessed 15 December 2015).

Fallon, P (Chair) (1999) *Report of the Committee of Inquiry into the Personality Disorder Unit, Ashworth Special Hospital*. London: TSO.

Fernando, S, Ndegwa, D and Wilson, M (1998) *Forensic Psychiatry, Race and Culture*. London: Routledge.

Gilroy, P (2002) *There Ain't No Black in the Union Jack*. London: Routledge.

Hawton, K, Linsell, L, Adeniji, T, Sariaslan, A and Fazel, S (2014) Self-harm in Prisons in England and Wales: An Epidemiological Study of Prevalence, Risk Factors, Clustering, and Subsequent Suicide. *The Lancet*, 383(9923): 1147–54.

Healthcare Commission (2007) *Count Me In Census*. London: Healthcare Commission.

HM Chief Inspector of Prisons for England and Wales (2014) *Annual Report 2013–14*. London: HMSO.

Liebling, A (1994) Suicide Amongst Women Prisoners. *The Howard Journal of Criminal Justice*, 33(1): 1–9.

Ministry of Justice (2009) Guidance for Social Supervisors [online]. Available at: www.justice.gov.uk/downloads/offenders/mentally-disordered-offenders/guidance-for-social-supervisors-0909.pdf (accessed 15 December 2015).

Ministry of Justice (2015) Safety in Custody Statistics England and Wales [online]. Available at: www.gov.uk/government/uploads/system/uploads/attachment_data/file/449648/safety-in-custody-2015.pdf (accessed 15 December 2015).

Plugge, E, Douglas, N and Fitzpatrick, R (2008) Patients, Prisoners, or People? Women Prisoners' Experiences of Primary Care in Prison: A Qualitative Study. *British Journal of General Practice*, 58: 630–6.

Prins, H (2010) *Offenders, Deviants or Patients? Explorations in Clinical Criminology* (4th edition). Hove: Routledge.

Rivlin, A, Hawton, K, Marzano, L and Fazel, S (2010) Psychiatric Disorders in Male Prisoners Who Made Near-lethal Suicide Attempts: Case-control Study. *The British Journal of Psychiatry*, 197(4): 313–19.

Tudor Hart, J (1971) The Inverse Care Law. *The Lancet*, 297(7696): 405–12.

5 Policing and Mental Illness

Critical questions

- **What has the phrase the 'criminalisation of the mentally ill' come to mean?**
- **What led Lord Adebowale to describe mental health issues as 'core police business'?**
- **What legal and policy safeguards does PACE provide to vulnerable adults in custody?**
- **What are the keys issues that arise in the use of section 136 MHA 1983?**

This chapter will explore the main argument put forward that the police have a key role to play in mental health services. The chapter examines the legislation and policy framework including section 136 MHA 1983 and the operation of PACE (2004), with the special protections that it offers to those in custody who are experiencing mental distress. The chapter concludes with a discussion of recent policy developments such as mental health triage.

Community care and policing

The combined effect of the shifts and changes outlined in Chapter 2's short history of community care has been termed the 'criminalisation of the mentally ill' (Aboleda-Florez and Holley, 1998). Borzecki and Wormith (1985) argue that for this thesis to hold, two conditions need to apply: there need to be higher levels of contact between mentally ill people and the police than the wider population; and the arrest rate for those experiencing mental health problems would have to be shown to be higher. Hartford et al's (2005) study is a statistical analysis of police recordings of contacts and responses to calls in Ontario. The study confirmed the greater risk that people with mental health problems face in contacts with the police. There are two elements to this: the mentally ill were more likely to come into contact with the police; and the result of this contact was shown to be more likely to result in custody. These findings have been supported in a range of studies which demonstrate that the mentally ill are: more likely to come into contact with the police; have a higher arrest rate; are at a greater risk of entering custody than being granted bail; and are more likely to be arrested for relatively minor offences (Teplin, 1984; Roberston, Pearson and Gibb, 1995).

'Cop culture'

In terms of policing, one of the key areas that has to be considered is 'police culture'. Sackmann (1991) defines culture as 'the collective construction of social reality'. A great deal of the analysis of policing focuses on 'cop culture'. There are a number of difficulties with using 'cop culture' instrumentally. Chan (1996) argues that occupational culture is not monolithic and cop culture for Chan is 'poorly defined and of little analytical value'. In fact, Manning (1993) argues that there are clear differences between 'street cop culture' and 'management culture'. The term 'cop culture' can be viewed as a label for a form of hegemonic masculinity (Carrigan et al, 1985) found in police settings. The major themes here would be: an emphasis on action as a solution to problems; and a strong sense of group identity and hyper-masculinity, manifesting in a series of misogynistic and racist attitudes. These attitudes would also include stereotypical views of the mentally ill and the idea that dealing with psychiatric emergencies was not 'proper policing'. In this schema, the police are hard-bitten, cynical and need to be aggressive to deal with the dangers that they face on a day-to-day basis. Reiner (2000b) links the development of these cultural attitudes to the demands of police work itself, rather than to their arising out of the wider society. Goldsmith (1990) suggests that these cultural attitudes are part of a functional response to the demands of the post.

Waddington (1999) takes issue with the way that 'canteen culture' has been used uncritically. For Waddington, the culture of the police canteen is, very importantly, an oral one. As he suggests, there is a gap between rhetoric and action. Despite the ongoing portrayal of police work as dynamic and exciting, the majority of it is not. To take one example, murder investigations involve a great deal of checking information, gathering statements and looking at tapes from CCTV, rather than the psychological profiling and car chases of the popular imagination. Loftus (2008) has noted how enduring these traits of police occupational culture are, despite a raft of changes that one might expect to dislodge them – for example, the recruitment of a more diverse workforce and greater public scrutiny and management moves to tackle these issues.

Mental health work as 'core police business'

Police officers can have a key role to play in situations in which individuals are experiencing some sort of crisis related to mental health problems. The Sainsbury Centre's (2008) study suggested that up to 15% of incidents dealt with by the police include some sort of mental health issue or concern. It also calls for the exercise of a range of skills. In his recent report, Lord Adebowale (2013) described mental health issues as 'core police business'. The police have considerable discretion in terms of their response (Bittner, 1967a). They may well be the emergency service that is first contacted by the relatives of those in acute distress, who are, for example, putting themselves or others at risk. If a person is acutely distressed in a public place, then the likelihood of some form of police involvement is increased significantly.

Despite the fact that this is a very important facet of day-to-day police work, it is an area that is neglected in police training (Cummins, 2007; 2008; 2010). Pinfold et al (2003) suggest that police officers hold a number of stereotypical views about mental illness, with the idea that there is a link between mental illness and violence being the most strongly held. This viewpoint is supported by Cotton (2004). As a result, the professional skills and knowledge that they acquire is largely through experience on duty or from their senior colleagues. This is an issue that has to be a common feature in policing in the industrialised world since the asylum closure programme began (Sims and Symonds, 1975; Tesse and van Wormer, 1975; Fry et al, 2002).

Janus et al's (1980) study shows that the benefits of training include increased empathy on the part of officers for those experiencing mental health problems. Cummins and Jones (2010) highlight the benefits of a different approach to the training of police officers. The Dyfed and Powys force developed a new model, which involved spending time on mental health units and receiving training from mental health staff and service user groups. This model of training has been very successful; the feedback from both police officers and mental health service users emphasised that this approach helps to challenge stereotypical views.

In the UK, successive governments, as outlined in the circulars 66/90 and 12/95 (Home Office, 1990; 1995) have followed a policy of diversion of the mentally ill from the CJS. The police station could be a key locus for this diversion or, perhaps more accurately, the accessing of mental health care. The provision has been patchy and has led to frustration for police officers (Vaughan et al, 2001; Curran and Matthews, 2001). However, access to appropriate mental health services for those in contact with the CJS, as the Bradley Report (2009) showed, is still fragmented and disjointed.

Policing always involves an element of discretion and individual judgement. This is particularly the case regarding working with individuals who are acutely distressed. Individual officers have to make a decision on how to exercise their legal powers or deal with the matter in some other way. Policing is about more than the detection of crime or apprehension of offenders; Wolff (2005) has gone further and suggests that police officers have always had a quasi-social work function in this field. However, as Husted et al (1995) argue, this is not something their training or police culture values highly. The conventional methods of co-ordinating services have not been successful (Wolff, 1998), and these problems are not limited to North America and Europe (Kimhi et al, 1998).

Police officers often have a significant role to play in mental health services, and MIND (2007) highlights the negative impact of such police involvement from the perspective of those using mental health services. Lamb et al (2002) provide a rationale in terms of public protection for police involvement, a role that has been expanded by the failure to develop robust community-based services in the era of deinstitutionalisation (Pogrebin, 1986). This adds to the well-documented frustration that police officers feel when dealing with mental health services (Graham, 2001).

Police officers in Gillig et al's (1990) study felt that what they really needed was access to information about an individual's past history as well as rapid support from mental health staff. This finding was supported by Stevenson et al (2011). Interestingly, in this study, mental health service users assumed that agencies shared information as a matter of course. Watson et al (2004a) find that knowledge of an individual's mental health history has a negative impact on how the police respond – in this study, the police were less likely to take action on the information provided if the individual had a history of mental illness. However, there is evidence that the police have skills in this area (Smith, 1990; Watson et al 2004b). This should not be a surprise as police officers are practised at dealing with distressed individuals in a wide variety of settings or situations.

Mental health issues in the custody setting

PACE and the role of the custody sergeant

PACE (2004) provides key safeguards for the protection of vulnerable adults – that is, adults with mental health problems or learning disabilities – while in police custody. Along with the standard procedures and rights such as the provision of legal advice and the taping of interviews, such individuals have to be interviewed with an appropriate adult present. Custody sergeants have a key role to play in this process as they, in effect, carry out a risk assessment of every individual who comes into custody. Advice on ensuring the safety of those with mental health problems forms part of the *Guidance on the Safer Detention and Handling of Persons in Police Custody* (ACPO, 2006). However, the guidance itself is not comprehensive. In any event, for it to be followed successfully, it is dependent on police officers making appropriate assessments of individuals' mental health needs. All individuals coming into police custody are assessed as to whether they are fit to be detained. Custody sergeants will carry out an initial screening exercise seeking medical or other support as required. This is a fluid process, but the initial decisions that are made are very influential.

There has been little research into the specific role of the custody sergeant under PACE (2004). Studies that have examined the role of the appropriate adult involve an indirect consideration of the custody sergeant role. However, there is not a specific study which explores the assessment of mental illness by police officers in this setting. Skinns's (2011) study of two custody suites does not consider the assessment of mental health issues by custody officers in any depth. The matter is referred to in a section looking at the way that the police work with volunteers acting as appropriate adults. Skinns suggests that this assessment is carried out in conjunction with a doctor. This is not always the case – under PACE, a formal medical assessment is not required for an appropriate adult to be involved.

The Confait case and the 1981 Royal Commission

Maxwell Confait was found murdered in his bedsit in London in 1972. He had been strangled and the bedsit set on fire. In November 1972, three youths – Colin Lattimore (18), Ronnie Leighton (15) and Amhet Salih (14) – were all convicted of arson with intent to endanger life. Colin Lattimore was also found guilty of manslaughter. Ronnie Leighton was convicted of murder. The basis of the prosecution case against all three was confession evidence. They appealed against convictions in July 1973; these appeals were unsuccessful. In June 1975, the cases were referred to the Court of Appeal; in October that year, the convictions were quashed (Fisher, 1977). The successful appeals were followed by a Royal Commission that reported in 1981. The changes that the Commission recommended were incorporated into PACE (1984). The investigation into the murder of Maxwell Confait took place in a different cultural and political climate to the one that now exists. In one sense, the image of British policing was largely one of a community-based force. Another obvious difference was the fact that interviews were not at that time tape recorded. Police interviews were governed by the 'Judges' Rules' and the CJS had yet to experience the shocks caused by a series of miscarriages of justice. The confessions in the Confait case were obtained under duress – a recurring feature in a series of miscarriages of justice in the 1970s and 1980s.

Vulnerable groups in custody

The introduction of PACE led to wider protections for those being interviewed by the police. The 'Judges Rules' were abolished and a new framework, including the tape recording of interviews, established. Three groups – juveniles, adults with learning difficulties and adults with mental health problems – were afforded additional protections. It was felt that such individuals were at particular risk of self-incrimination. This is an example of the influence of the welfare model having an impact on the development of the CJS. On the whole, these measures have been widely accepted and are regarded as legitimate, although in the recent policy debates concerning the CJS, the role of the appropriate adult has not featured.

PACE safeguards

Section 66 PACE ensures that special safeguards exist when the police are questioning or interviewing people with mental health problems. Evidence that has been obtained under duress can be excluded from any trial (section 76(2)(a)). There are further provisions in section 76 and section 78 PACE (1984), which relate to the admissibility of confession evidence obtained from vulnerable adults. The Confait case and subsequent work by psychologists such as Gudjonsson and MacKeith (1997) have established that vulnerable adults can be pressurised into making confession statements. Such statements can have a very powerful influence on the subsequent progress of the case, particularly on the decision any jury makes, and have been a feature of several miscarriages of justice, the Judith Ward case being one such example. Judith Ward was convicted in 1974 of the M62 terrorist bombing of a coach taking soldiers back to barracks. As was eventually demonstrated at her appeal in 1992, Ward suffered from mental health problems. She had retracted her confession at the time of the original trial, but the prosecution case was still based on sections of it (see www.lrb.co.uk/v15/n21/paul-foot/still-it-goes-on).

The role of the appropriate adult under PACE (2004)

I will now go on to examine the role of the appropriate adult in practice before considering the development of case law and wider considerations of its efficacy. As noted above, the decision to involve an appropriate adult rests, in effect, with the custody officer. When a professional has been contacted by the police, they have to decide if they are best placed to take on the role. It is possible that they will be excluded because of some knowledge of the offence. On a wider issue, we have seen that the involvement of an appropriate adult can be a somewhat haphazard affair. It is possible that a mental health team is contacted when a professional from a learning disabilities background would have skills more relevant to the case. I recognise that in some areas, the idea that there might be a choice of who will act as an appropriate adult will be seen as utopian. However, it is a factor to be considered. When taking the referral, the appropriate adult should obtain as much information from the police as possible. This would include: the nature of the alleged offence; the grounds for regarding the person as a vulnerable adult; the timescale of the arrest and proposed interview; and whether legal representation has been sought. Code C (para 3.13) indicates that the appropriate adult can override the person's decision to refuse legal representation. This might be seen as an example of paternalism and the infantilisation of vulnerable adults.

Acting as an appropriate adult

On arrival at the police station, the appropriate adult should check the information that they have been given already and examine the custody record. An important point to consider is the role of the forensic physician. In such circumstances, the person in custody should be assessed as to whether they are 'fit to be interviewed'. This is not the same judgement as to whether an appropriate adult should be involved.

An individual in custody should be informed of their rights, which are as follows:

- the right to have someone informed that they are there;

- free legal advice;

- the right to consult the PACE Codes of Practice and to have a copy of the custody record.

(PACE 2004, Code C para 3.1)

The appropriate adult should ensure that the individual is given their rights in their presence along with an explanation of the caution. In this initial period, the appropriate adult can clarify any issues relating to the initial arrest and detention.

Code C (para 3) ensures that the appropriate adult has the right to consult privately with the detained person. The appropriate adult does not enjoy legal privilege in the way that a solicitor would do; they need to explain their role without becoming involved in discussion of the case, as this might compromise their position to fulfil the role. The appropriate adult should assess the vulnerability of the person, and this can be another stage in the filters of diversion from custody. One of the reasons for involving the appropriate adult is because of their specialist skills and knowledge. I would contend that this is one of the strongest arguments for social workers taking on the role. Social workers with experience in mental health settings will have developed assessment skills. It is possible that an individual could be diverted from the CJS at this stage or that an MHA assessment is arranged. The appropriate adult has to ensure that the person understands the process of interviewing. In addition, this would be the opportunity to raise any concerns that the person has about the detention.

During the interview, the appropriate adult should ensure that it is conducted properly and fairly and facilitate communication (Code C para 11.16). The appropriate adult has a key role in ensuring that the interview does not become 'oppressive'. Given the acknowledged vulnerability of this group, as noted above, this is an area that calls for heightened awareness of the issues involved. PACE (1984) established the tape recording of interviews so the appropriate adult has to state their name and role at the beginning of the tape. In addition to the conduct of the interview, the appropriate adult has to ensure that the person is aware that they have the right of access to the tape recording. The appropriate adult should be an active participant in the interview, not an observer. In addition, they can make representations at any review of the detention. The appropriate adult should witness any other procedures that follow the interview, for example the taking of samples, fingerprinting and photographs (Code D paras 1.11–14). The appropriate adult's role extends to witnessing any caution or charging (Code C para 16.1). They also have the right to request copies of the custody record and tape recordings of the interview. In some cases, further interviews may be required, so it will be necessary to ensure that an appropriate adult is present. If the person is to remain in custody, it is important that information is provided to the prison, so that their mental health needs are highlighted. The appropriate adult needs to make comprehensive notes as they might be called to Court at a later date. In addition, this might assist in future risk assessment or care planning.

How effective is the appropriate adult role?

The role of the appropriate adult is full of contradictions. It was introduced with the clear intention of providing an increased level of protection within the CJS for groups that were seen as being particularly vulnerable. The legal system in England and Wales is an adversarial one. The appropriate adult's role is somewhere in the middle of the conflict between the suspect and the officers. I should make it clear that the role of the appropriate adult also exists to support vulnerable people when they are witnesses. This is a very important area, but I am only concerned with the issues raised by appropriate adults' involvement in the interviews of suspects. I will examine the extent to which appropriate adults are present at interviews, who performs the role, how effective appropriate adults are and the case law that has arisen since the introduction of PACE (1984).

Robertson, Pearson and Gibb (1995) carried out a study of how people with mental health problems came into contact with the CJS. This was an observational study based at London police stations and Courts. In the study, 37 suspects (1.4%, n=2721) were considered 'actively mentally ill'. This sample highlighted that those who were mentally ill were more likely to have been arrested for a violent offence. The most common diagnosis was schizophrenia (25). Officers only formally interviewed 30% of the sample (822 suspects). In this group, ten were considered to be mentally ill. However, appropriate adults were present for only five of the interviews. The study argues that the decision to involve an appropriate adult in these cases was related to the serious nature of the offence – the implication being that the police were more careful to ensure procedural accuracy in such cases, as officers wanted to avoid the interviews being ruled inadmissible. The level of involvement of appropriate adults in PACE (1984) interviews does not appear to correlate with the increased contact between the police and people with mental health problems, and the levels of mental illness in the general population. A range of factors are at play here, including lack of awareness of mental health issues and organisational difficulties in the provision of appropriate services. It is argued that the police have a vested interest in not ensuring that the provisions of PACE (1984) are applied: as well as the practical difficulties, in an adversarial system, involving an appropriate adult might be seen as giving the suspect an unnecessary advantage. Studies by Bean and Nemitz (1994) and Clare and Gudjonsson (1992) found similarly low levels of involvement of appropriate adults.

The role of the appropriate adult is a complex and demanding one; it requires a mix of skills and knowledge. These would include an understanding of the legal process and ideally some specialist mental health knowledge. Guidance 1E advises that a trained appropriate adult is the best choice. However, as the Home Office (2002) review makes clear, this is often not the case. The role of the appropriate adult is taken on by volunteers, carers, relatives and professionals. In Medford et al (2003) a doorman even took on this role. As White (2002) argues, this situation is fraught with possible complications and an untrained appropriate adult may do more harm than good. In addition, it is important to recognise that individuals, even professionals, can find the situation of the PACE (1984) interview intimidating.

Ensuring that an interview is conducted fairly and in a non-oppressive manner will inevitably include situations requiring professionals to challenge police conduct. Harkin (1997) indicates that, as even social workers find custody suites intimidating, it is probable that this will be even more so for those working in a voluntary capacity. As noted above, the appropriate adult has a key role to play; however, no official qualifications or training are required for those carrying out the role. The disjointed nature of service and training provision was noted by the Runciman Commission in 1993.

Some legal questions to consider

Because the appropriate adult does not enjoy legal privilege in the way that a defence solicitor would, it is therefore possible that they will be called as a witness at a subsequent trial. The most famous example of this was the trial of Rosemary West. Janet Leach, who acted as appropriate adult for the interviews of Fred West, was called to give evidence. This is clearly a very unusual example indeed, but does highlight the ambiguous nature of the role. The case law that has grown surrounding the appropriate adult has largely been concerned with the suitability of the person taking on the role. In *DPP v Blake*, it was found that the estranged father of a juvenile should not have taken on the role because he was not sufficiently neutral. On different grounds, it was held that the father in *R v Morse* should not have acted as an appropriate adult because his low IQ score meant that he could not understand the serious nature and wide scope of the role. However, a subsequent decision in *R v Cox* confuses this point. In the Cox case, a mother with both a learning difficulty and severe mental health problems acted as the appropriate adult. If she had been the suspect, she would not have been interviewed without an appropriate adult – yet the confession evidence of her daughter was deemed admissible. Such decisions do not appear to chime with the underlying reasons for the introduction of the role and might serve to reduce the role to a purely administrative function, rather than a cornerstone of attempts to protect vulnerable people. The decision in *R v Aspinall* made it clear that the role of the appropriate adult is to safeguard the suspect's rights, but this is in addition to – not instead of – the solicitor's role in this process. Bartlett and Sandland (2003) argue that the details of the role the appropriate adult should play are still unclear. They see that at the heart of this confusion are what the terms 'facilitate communication' and 'fair interview' actually mean. In mental health cases, for example, can social workers really be neutral if they have previously assessed an individual under MHA (1983)? As they rightly point out in juvenile cases, the PACE interview itself can be the point of a family conflict that means the parents are not neutral at all.

Discussion

The final area I wish to consider is the effectiveness of the appropriate adult role and an examination of who actually carries out this role. The appropriate adult is a specialist role but it is not necessarily one that social workers perform on a regular basis. This serves to make it difficult to build up the skills, practice and confidence required to perform the role well. Brown, Ellis and Larcombe (1992) found that the police were actually happier for social workers to take on this role. This is despite a general lack of confidence in mental health services and might indicate that if services can be delivered properly, and in a timely fashion, organisational suspicion can be reduced. These findings contrast with Pierpoint's (2000) study of the use of volunteers as appropriate adults in juvenile cases. In this study, volunteers were more effective. This probably reflects the family tensions and the difficult position for social workers in these cases. Research has highlighted the fact that, on too many occasions, the appropriate adult does little more than act as a passive observer during interviews; this was the case in Evans's (1993) study of interviews involving juveniles. The appropriate adult has a wider role in the custody process – for example, ensuring that a suspect understands their rights and has appropriate breaks and, as noted above, the appropriate adult can override a decision to refuse legal representation. These are areas of the role that need to be explored further.

The role of the appropriate adult is an attempt to offer additional protection to a very vulnerable group; however, it is difficult to disagree with the Home Office's review of PACE (2002), which indicated that the present provision for Appropriate Adult services was very patchy indeed, and 'chaotic and unstructured'. It recommended the establishment of a national policy and full national guidance for the scheme.

There are several themes that emerge in the literature; the first concerns the relatively limited involvement of the appropriate adult throughout the custody process. The extent and complexity of the mental health needs of the prison population have been well established, and one would expect there to be similar levels of need among those whom the police arrest, as the groups are likely to share many characteristics. There does not appear to be any substantial evidence that large numbers are being diverted from the CJS at any early stage. There may be arguments about the causes, but it is generally agreed that the police have more contact with people with mental health problems. This trend is difficult to reverse and will remain a feature of police work for the foreseeable future. As Stone (1982) argues, medicine and other disciplines have never been able to develop a coherent strategy for dealing with the mentally ill who commit criminal offences. The barriers to the development of such a policy in terms of philosophical agreement, resources and the support of the wider population remain deeply entrenched. The result has been a series of shifts between placing the emphasis on punishment, treatment or a mixture of both. Stone's comments were made in a review of works examining seventeenth-century society; however, they remain relevant to current debates.

In examining the role of the appropriate adult, some fundamental questions need to be considered – the first and most fundamental being whether the role can be justified. The research reviewed above suggests that in many cases, the appropriate adult acts as a passive observer of the proceedings and contributes very little. Medford et al's study (2003), in which records of interviews were analysed, includes interviews with vulnerable adults and juvenile suspects. The study highlighted that social workers and volunteers are more likely to take on the role in adult cases, while family members or parents often acted as appropriate adults for juveniles. It is interesting to note that the appropriate adult was more likely to intervene in the juvenile cases, with some of the family interventions being inappropriate – for example, encouraging a juvenile to confess. This is supported by Pierpoint (2000), who argues that volunteers are more effective and often offer more protection in interviews with juveniles. These studies highlight the danger that the role of the appropriate adult can become a largely administrative one with little contribution being made. However, Medford et al (2003) conclude that the presence of the appropriate adult has an important effect on police behaviour. In interviews with adults, it increases the likelihood that legal representation is sought; this, in itself must be a positive for the interests of justice. The study also indicates that the legal representative will be more forceful in such cases – the overall effect is that the interview is less aggressive. This is the result of a combination of factors, such as the police wanting to ensure that they are procedurally correct and that such interviews cannot be challenged at a later date. It should be noted that studies of the interventions that appropriate adults make concentrate on the interview – which is not that surprising – although the role is wider than this, including examining the custody record, possibly seeking legal representation and overriding the wishes of the suspect and ensuring that the person in custody understands their rights. One could carry out all these tasks and not necessarily intervene in the actual interview. However, the general conclusion that too many appropriate adults remain passive observers is still valid.

A root-and-branch reform that would remove the role of the appropriate adult would serve to increase the vulnerability of a very marginalised group. The general thrust of the PACE review in this area is that the police need more support from mental health services. While the primary function of the appropriate adult is not one of diversion, to remove this layer of support would make it more difficult for police officers and could put individuals at increased risk. White (2002) argues for legal privilege to be extended to those taking on the role of the appropriate adult. I find it difficult to establish the benefits of such a change, for it involves a fundamental shift in the balance of the role. In the adversarial legal system, the appropriate adult would shift from the current neutral to an almost representative function. The problems that have been highlighted revolve around the training and skills that individuals being asked to take on the role have. Fennell (1994) argues that the way to ensure that those with mental health problems are offered adequate protections is to develop a group of legal representatives with specialist knowledge and skills in this area. Members of the group would then be called in such cases, which would negate the need for an appropriate adult. Such a scheme would require a significant investment in the training of legal representatives and a commitment from the legal profession; it also involves a philosophical shift. I would suggest that the combination of the roles would be very difficult if not impossible.

I would argue that the provisions of PACE (1984) do provide valuable safeguards for vulnerable suspects; however, the current practice position raises concerns. It is clear that the policies of deinstitutionalisation and bed closure have not been adequately supported by appropriately increased community resources. This view appeared to be shared by the New Labour administration in *Modernising Mental Health Services* (Department of Health, 1998). While few would dispute that the aim of 'diversion from custody' is a laudable one, the current evidence is that this policy has not succeeded. There is evidence from James (2000) and McGilloway and Donnelly (2004) that early diversion schemes can be effective. In both studies, community psychiatric nurses were attached to police stations to divert those involved in minor offences and attempt to engage this difficult-to-reach group with mental health care services. There is a moral justification for the support of such policies in the idea of equivalence – those in custody should receive the same level of health care as other members of society. In addition, such services may help to prevent repeat offending or an escalation in the level of offences committed. Some jurisdictions in the United States have introduced mental health courts to try to tackle this issue. The PACE review calls for the development of such schemes and for greater health care involvement at police stations. The triage schemes discussed in this chapter are an example of the sort of services that need to be developed further. I would argue that there is a need for an interprofessional approach so that staff from medical and social care backgrounds are involved in the development and provision of such services. The review goes on to consider other wide-reaching suggestions such as 'cell-blocking' charges and the development of more secure unit provision, although the majority of offenders would not need this level of security.

White (2002) argues that there is confusion about the exact nature of the role of the appropriate adult and the best way to protect vulnerable suspects in police custody. The judgment in *R v Lewis* indicates that the role overlaps with the legal representative and includes ensuring that the vulnerable suspect fully understands their legal rights. In addition to this quasi-legal role, there is a welfare role. The Code of Practice indicates that ideally this role will be taken on by a mental health professional. In Bucke and Brown's study (1997), it was found that social workers took on the role in 60% of cases, while Evans and Rawstorne (1994) highlight the fact that social services departments were better at providing social workers to take on this during the standard office hours. It is clearly more logistically difficult when emergency duty teams are covering an area as there are fewer staff, who have to cover a wider range of service provision.

It is important to remember that the Royal Commission that led to PACE (1984) has its roots in a grave miscarriage of justice. As Haley and Swift (1988) argue, the ultimate aim of these safeguards is to try to reduce the risk of unreliable evidence – but this has not been achieved in all cases. Justice (justice.org.uk) produced a report in 1994 which highlighted cases where miscarriages of justice followed vulnerable suspects giving unreliable statements.

Williams (2000) argues that there is a need for wider training for those who act in the role of the appropriate adult. This lack of a consistent approach had been identified by the Royal Commission (1993) and the insufficiency of confidence and expertise is not limited to non-professional staff who take on the role. Harkin (1997) discusses this in terms of social workers' experiences and suggests that social workers can find the whole experience isolating and intimidating. The ambiguous nature of the role, the legal knowledge required and the fact that, for many, this is not a regular working occurrence serve to make this an area of difficult social work practice. As it stands, there are no formal qualifications required for taking on this role. The National Appropriate Adult Network (www.appropriateadult.org.uk) is working to produce a set of national standards which will govern the recruitment, selection and supervision of all those who will take on the role.

Whatever systems and policies are put in place, they will still be dependent on the skills and professionalism of individual police officers. As noted above, officers often feel that they lack skills in this area and do not have a great deal of faith in the efficacy of mental health service interventions. In addition, in an adversarial system, they are not encouraged to do anything that will help the other side: if an officer does not recognise that an individual has a mental health problem, they will not put any policy aimed at protecting vulnerable individuals into place.

Section 136 MHA

Background

Section 136 MHA is a police power: it authorises any police officer to remove someone, who appears to be mentally disordered, from a publicly accessible place to a 'place of safety'. This is an emergency power and is generally used in circumstances where a person is putting themselves at immediate risk. Examples would include people who are threatening suicide or someone who is behaving in a very disturbed or disinhibited fashion. The use of section 136 MHA relies on the assessment of the individual police officers involved – there is no need for a formal medical diagnosis – and its purpose is for a mental health assessment to be carried out by a psychiatrist and an AMHP at the 'place of safety', which should normally be a hospital although it can be a police cell, but this is widely recognised as being far from ideal (this is discussed in more detail below). The section lasts up to 72 hours; however, the MHA Code of Practice and locally agreed protocols emphasise that these assessments should be completed as quickly as possible. The recent Home Office review of section 136 recommends that this time limit be reduced to 24 hours – this is the case with the equivalent Scottish legislation – and many Mental Health Trusts have developed section 136 suites at mental health units to tackle these issues.

The use of section 136 MHA

The monitoring of the use of section 136 has been generally poor; however, it is widely accepted that there has been an increase in its use over the past 20 years. There is a body of literature (Rogers and Faulkner, 1987; Dunn and Fahy, 1987; Bhui et al, 2003) that highlights the over-representation of BME groups, particularly young black men, in section 136 detentions. This is a crucial issue, as it means that in a number of cases the first contact that this group has with mental health services is via the police or other areas of the CJS. Section 136 MHA is much more likely to take place outside of standard office hours when normal support services are more widely available. Borschmann (2010) indicates that the 'typical' section 136 patient is a young, single, working-class male with a past history of mental illness – a group which is much less likely than others in the population to access general health care, including mental health services. Borschmann's study also noted that this group tended not to be registered with a GP. The Independent Police Complaints Commission carried out a major study of the use of section 136 in 2005/6 (IPCC, 2006). In this study, 11,500 patients were assessed in custody and 5900 in a mental health setting. The report highlighted significant variations between forces; some of these can be explained by local conditions – for example, Sussex police covers Beachy Head, a well-known 'suicide spot'. This study also confirmed Browne's (2009) finding that black people were almost twice as likely as other groups to be subject to section 136.

Use of police cells as a place of safety

Police custody is a pressurised, busy and often chaotic environment – there is clearly the potential for this to have a negative impact on an individual's mental health. As I have discussed in previous research (Cummins, 2007; 2008; Cummins and Jones, 2010) police officers are called upon to manage very difficult situations, such as self-harm or attempted suicide, often with little training or support. The physical environment of a police cell also needs to be taken into account when considering the potential impact of custody. A police cell should only be used as a place of safety in exceptional circumstances. Hampson (2011) argues that in practice, 'exceptional' means that the patient is 'too disturbed to be managed elsewhere'. HM Inspectorate of Constabulary's 2013 study *A Criminal Use of Police Cells?* examined in detail 70 cases where a cell had been used as a place of safety. At the time of writing, it is estimated that 36% of all section 136 detentions involve the use of police custody. There are significant variations between or even within forces – this is the result of different local service provision. The most common reason for a police cell being used was that the person was drunk and/or violent or had a history of violence.

Service user perspectives

There is very limited research which examines service user perspectives on the experience of being detained under section 136. As the HMIC review notes, the experience can be – if the individual is taken to police custody – almost the same as being arrested. In custody, they are treated in the same way as any other person; the booking-in process is the same – and it would include being searched. On occasions, because of concerns about self-harm or suicide, clothing may be taken away from the detained person. There will almost certainly be periods of delay – in custody or in an accident and emergency department. Jones and Mason's (2002) study highlighted that, from a service user perspective, this is a custodial not a therapeutic experience. In this study, participants made it clear that the routine of being booked into custody was a dehumanising one. They also felt that police officers were too quick to assess that they were at risk of self-harm, meaning that there was an increased prospect of being placed in a paper suit (Riley et al (2011) confirm this dissatisfaction with the process). In particular, the service users in the study felt that they were being treated like criminals for experiencing distress; and some felt that their mental health had worsened because of their time in custody.

MS v UK

The case of *MS v UK*, which was decided in the European Court of Human Rights (ECHR) in 2012, demonstrates the potential difficulties that can arise. MS was detained under section 136 MHA following an assault on a relative. When he was assessed at the police station, it was decided that he needed to be transferred to psychiatric care. There then followed a series of delays and arguments between mental health services as to which unit would be the most appropriate to meet MS's mental health needs. This argument went on for so long that the 72-hour limit of section 136 MHA was passed. MS was still in police custody and this had a dramatic impact on his mental state; for example, as a result of paranoid delusional ideas, he refused food. The ECHR held that the treatment of MS constituted a breach of article 3, which prohibits inhumane and degrading treatment. This is clearly an unusual case, but it illustrates the potential issues that arise. While the judgment made it clear that the initial decision to detain MS under mental health legislation was valid and justified, it is clear that the police cannot hope to tackle the root causes of these problems in isolation (see www. mentalhealthlaw.co.uk/MS_v_UK_24527/08_(2012)_ECHR_804,_(2012)_MHLO_46).

Outcomes

The HSCIC data (see www.hscic.gov.uk/dars) shows that in the majority of cases, those individuals assessed following the police use of section 136 were not formally admitted to hospital – that is, they were detained under sections 2 or 3 of the MHA 1983. One of the major difficulties when examining the use of section 136 is the danger that there is too narrow a focus on outcomes. It is a fallacy to argue that section 136 has not been used appropriately if the person is not detained; the test of section 136 is whether the officer thinks 'that it is necessary to do so in the interests of that person or for the protection of others'. Police officers have to respond to the emergency that they face; if mental health professionals carry out an assessment and alternatives to hospital are organised, then that does not mean the police officer's decision was incorrect. The whole purpose of section 136 is for an assessment to be carried out, not for a formal admission to hospital. Borschmann's 2010 study, an analysis of the implementation of section 136 in a South London Trust, shows that 41.2% of these uses did not lead to hospital admission, while 34.4% led to admission under the MHA and 23.1% to an informal admission.

The use of section 136 MHA raises very important civil liberty issues as well as wider ones about the treatment of people experiencing mental health problems. As Latham (1997) points out, it allows for an individual to detain someone; and unlike sections 5(2) and 5(4) of the MHA, the person with this power has no medical training, and no medical evidence is required for the power to be enacted. In fact, while the purpose of detention under section 136 is for psychiatric assessment, it is important to bear in mind, however, that this is just one area of mental health work in which police officers are potentially involved. There is a danger that controversies about the working of section 136 overshadow the whole debate in this field.

Mental health emergencies, triage and models of policing

This section will examine the ways in which policing has responded to the pressures of mental health work. It begins with a discussion of the ideas that underpin triage, and it then goes on to examine the way that this concept has been adapted to the field of policing and mental health.

Triage

Triage is a very well-established practice in nursing. The fundamental idea of triage is a straightforward one: early assessment enables medical staff to identify those in greatest medical need, so that treatment and resources can be directed in the most effective fashion. Broadbent (2002) concludes that effective triage leads to better outcomes for patients. It is, of course, standard practice in accident and emergency departments. Mental health issues, though, do not fit easily into the standard model of triage (Clarke et al, 2007). The participants in this study voiced dissatisfaction with the service provided at accident and emergency; however, they felt that they had 'nowhere else to go' (p 128) if they were in crisis. One of the issues here is the nature of accident and emergency departments: they are busy, often seemingly chaotic. The noise and other factors, such as lack of privacy, make them far from ideal environments for anyone experiencing acute distress. In addition, mental health problems are complicated and messy – they are often the result of longstanding issues – and difficult to diagnose. The result is that accident and emergency is probably one of the worst environments that can be imagined in which to carry out these assessments. Mental health triage has come to be used as a shorthand for a number of joint mental health and police initiatives in this area; these schemes all try to bring police and mental health professionals together in a more effective way. One of the overall aims is to avoid the use of police custody and support police confidence in decision making.

Models of police triage

As outlined above, mental health is a key issue for policing. In a number of areas, police forces have developed new responses to try to tackle these longstanding issues. These models are often the result of a crisis or, increasingly in the UK, an attempt to deal with reduced resources and increased demand. Lamb et al (2002) suggest three broad models of police response, discussed below, which have been developed to respond to people in crisis. Because mental health crisis is a very wide term, it is not used in any clinical sense here.

Crisis Intervention Team (CIT)

This is probably the best known of the specialist models. The model was developed in Memphis following the fatal shooting by the police of a man who was experiencing an episode of psychosis. CIT established a system of specialist training for accredited officers. These officers then deal with mental health emergencies but are also available to offer specialist advice. The model has been adopted across the USA. One of the key factors in the success of this model is the fact that hospitals will accept all CIT referrals (Watson et al, 2008).

This is a model that is very specific to the US context – particularly given the much greater likelihood that such incidents will involve firearms.

Joint police and mental health teams

The most well-established of these models are to be found in North America – CAR 87 in Vancouver is an example of such a project. Police and mental health are available in a patrol car to respond to any mental health emergency. In early 2014, similar schemes were established in Birmingham and Leicester. Reuland et al (2009) note that there are organisational advantages here and also that the outcomes for patients are improved.

Phone triage

One of the key challenges that police officers face is having to make decisions with access to limited information or often no information at all. Phone triage is a way of overcoming some of these problems. Edmondson and Cummins (2014) evaluated one such scheme based in Oldham; GMP officers were able to contact a dedicated 24-hour telephone number for professional advice and assistance from the local Trust's psychiatric liaison service, when they believed somebody was suffering with mental health issues. It was found that the service resulted in quicker assessments for people affected by a mental health crisis, thereby reducing officer time.

Conclusion

Bittner (1970) famously summed up the role of the police officer as 'Florence Nightingale in pursuit of Willie Sutton' (Sutton was an infamous bank robber). Bittner's phrase encapsulates the increasingly bewildering range of tasks that have become police work; it has undoubtedly become more complicated over the past 40 years and police officers thus, as section 136 demonstrates, have a range of possible responses to any situation. Arrest and custody should be viewed as being at one end of a continuum. In Teplin's (1984) seminal study of policing and mental illness, she uses the term 'mercy booking' to describe the situation where the police arrest an individual because they felt that this would ensure that a vulnerable person would be given food and shelter – even if it was in custody. Morabito (2007) argues that police decision making is more complex than is allowed for in these situations; she argues that it is shaped by a number of variables, which she terms 'horizons of context', a model that provides a tool for the analysis of the decisions that officers make within which there are three variable contexts. The scenic context refers to the choice of the community resources that are available, including the range of voluntary and statutory mental health services, access to training for officers and the working relationships between agencies. The discretion that officers can exercise is clearly limited by the range of services available; if community services are limited, then custody becomes, regrettably, a more likely outcome.

As well as the community resources, Morabito outlines two other 'horizons of context', which she terms temporal and manipulative. In this model, temporal refers to the individual and manipulative to the actual incident. There will be some incidents – for example, in the rare cases when a violent crime has been committed – where the police, for evidential and public protection reasons, will have little alternative but to take the person into custody. At the other end of the scale, a very experienced officer dealing with a minor incident involving an individual they know well will have much greater scope to exercise discretion. The scope will increase in areas where there are greater community mental health resources. As Morabito concludes, there is a tendency to oversimplify the decision-making processes that police officers use in these complex and demanding situations. The local service, social and environmental contexts are thus vitally important.

The recent retrenchment in mental health and wider public services mean that the police face increasing demands in this area (Edmondson and Cummins, 2014). Police involvement in mental health work has to be viewed as part of their role in wider community safety and the protection of vulnerable people; for example, there is often not an immediate response in terms of action that can be taken. It is an area that does create particular challenges for police services (Carey, 2001; Lurigio and Watson, 2010) and these challenges are both individual and organisational. Police officers do not receive a great deal of training in this area (Cummins and Jones, 2010); in addition, there is well-documented frustration among the police about the shortcomings in community-based mental health services, and the potential impact that these have on their own role.

In February 2014, the *Mental Health Crisis Care Concordat* (www.crisiscareconcordat.org.uk) was signed by more than 20 national organisations in England in a bid to drive up standards of care for people in police custody. The Concordat sought to build on other announcements on mental health care; these have included liaison and diversion schemes – for example, placing mental health professionals in police custody and court settings to help identify mental health problems in offenders as early as possible. In addition, a number of areas have developed versions of street triage schemes where mental health clinicians – typically trained nurses – accompany police officers when making emergency responses to people suffering from a mental health crisis. The nurses may also advise and support officers by telephone. As the College of Policing Chief Executive, Chief Constable Alex Marshall, stated in 2014:

> *The Concordat is a strong statement of intent of how the police, mental health services, social work services and ambulance professionals will work together to make sure that people who need immediate mental health support at a time of crisis get the right services when they need them.*
>
> (www.college.police.uk/Pages/Home.aspx)

Wood et al's (2011) review of trends in the UK, Canada and the USA concludes that the same issues arise across the countries: a combination of reduced psychiatric provision and poorly funded community services has led to increased pressure on police officers, who often receive little or no specific mental health training. The police have increasingly found themselves part of both. In the UK, the wider policing agenda has meant that there has been a significant shift so that policing is concerned with more than the detection and arrest of offenders. Police officers, particularly in urban areas, deal with incidents that relate in some way or another to mental illness on an almost daily basis. It is likely that the police will always be 'first responders' to many incidents. The key, then, is to explore how the police are to be supported by wider community mental health agencies to ensure that their response is appropriate. This is not only to ensure that individuals are safe, but also to support police officers to make informed, professional and defensible decisions. There will always be cases where an individual who is mentally ill will be taken into police custody because they have committed or are suspected of a violent crime. These are the minority. Police officers need training in mental health awareness to increase their confidence in decision making; in addition, there needs to be more effective liaising and joint working between mental health services and the police to ensure that individuals receive support from the most appropriate services in a timely fashion.

Mental health and policing is moving up the policy agenda; this is a welcome development. The debates in this area need to include a consideration of possible reform of section 136 MHA, including ways of ensuring that police cells are not routinely used as places of safety. However, there is a danger that the focus on section 136 will push to the margins the wider role that police officers potentially have in this field. Lord Adebowale concluded that mental health is core police business; this should be taken to mean that dealing with individuals experiencing mental distress is a key feature of the working week of most police officers. There are a number of models of triage that have been developed in response to local organisational, demographic and other factors – for example, a response to a tragic incident or the commitment of individuals. Although it would be foolish to try to be very prescriptive in developing such models of triage, all these schemes do have two key features: the improved training for officers and improved liaison with mental health services. These elements are vital, whatever the nature of the mental health crisis or incident that is being addressed. My research shows the extent of the challenge that is faced; however, it also highlights that officers skilfully deal with complex and demanding situations – often with little specialist support – ensuring the safety and welfare of vulnerable citizens.

Taking it further

Adebowale, Lord (2013) *Independent Commission on Mental Health and Policing Report.* London: Independent Commission on Mental Health and Policing.

Borschmann, R D (2010) Demographic and Referral Patterns of People Detained Under Section 136 of the Mental Health Act (1983) in a South London Mental Health Trust from 2005 to 2008. *Medicine, Science and the Law,* 50(1): 15–18.

Bradley, K (2009) *The Bradley Report: Lord Bradley's Review of People with Mental Health Problems or Learning Disabilities in the Criminal Justice System.* London: Department of Health.

Broadbent, M (2002) Improving Competence in Emergency Mental Health Triage. *Accident and Emergency Nursing,* 10: 155–62.

Bucke, T and Brown, D (1997) *In Police Custody: Police Powers and Suspects' Rights Under the Revised PACE Codes of Practice.* London: Home Office Research Development and Statistics Directorate.

Carrigan, T, Connell, B and Lee, J (1985) Toward a New Sociology of Masculinity. *Theory and Society,* 5(14): 551–604.

Clarke, D, Dusome, D and Hughes, L (2007) Emergency Department from the Mental Health Client's Perspective. *International Journal of Mental Health Nursing,* 16: 126–31.

Cotton, D (2004) The Attitudes of Canadian Police Officers Toward the Mentally Ill. *International Journal of Law and Psychiatry*, 27(2): 135–46.

Edmondson, D and Cummins, I (2014) *Oldham Mental Health Phone Triage/RAID Pilot Project Evaluation Report* [online]. Available at: www.crisiscareconcordat.org.uk (accessed 15 December 2015).

Evans, R (1993) *The Conduct of Police Interviews with Juveniles* (Royal Commission on Criminal Justice Research Study 12). London: HMSO.

Evans, R and Rawstorne, S (1994) The Protection of Vulnerable Suspects (Report to the Home Office Research and Planning Unit), in Brown, D (1997), *PACE Ten Years On: A Review of the Research* (Home Office Research Study no 155). London: HMSO.

Hampson, M (2011) Raising Standards in Relation to Section 136 of the Mental Health Act 1983. *Advances in Psychiatric Treatment*, 11: 365–71.

Harkin, E (1997) *Acting as an Appropriate Adult for Suspects with Learning Difficulties* (Social Work Monograph 158), Norwich: University of East Anglia.

HMIC (2013) *A Criminal Use of Police Cells? The Use of Police Custody as a Place of Safety for People with Mental Health Needs* [online]. Available at: www.hmic.gov.uk (accessed 15 December 2015).

IPCC (2006) Police Custody as a 'Place of Safety': Examining the Use of Section 136 of the Mental Health Act 1983 [online]. Available at: www.ipcc.gov.uk/sites/default/files/Documents/guide-lines_reports/section_136.pdf (accessed 15 December 2015).

Loftus, B (2008) Dominant Culture, Interrupted Recognition, Resentment and the Politics of Change in an English Police Force. *British Journal of Criminology*, 48(6): 756–77.

Medford, S, Gudjonsson, G and Pearse, J (2003) The Efficacy of the Appropriate Adult Safeguard During Police Interviewing. *Legal and Criminological Psychology*, 8(2): 253–66.

MIND (2007) *Another Assault: MIND's Campaign for Equal Access to Justice for People with Mental Health Problems*. London: MIND.

Reuland, M, Schwarzfeld, M and Draper, L (2009) *Law Enforcement Responses to People With Mental Illnesses: A Guide to Research-informed Policy and Practice*. New York: Council of State Government's Justice Center.

Wood, J, Swanson, J, Burris, J D and Gilbert, A (2011) *Police Interventions with Persons Affected by Mental Illnesses: A Critical Review of Global Thinking and Practice*. New York: Rutgers University Center for Behavioral Health Services and Criminal Justice Research.

6 The Way Forward: Rediscovering Dignity

Critical questions

- *How do penal scholars explain the expansion of the use of imprisonment?*

- *What are the implications of Garland's phrase 'the decline of the rehabilitative ideal'?*

- *How can we use Hall's notion of conjuncture as a means of analysing the potential for reform of the penal system?*

- *What are the lessons to be learned from the US case of* **Brown v Plata?**

In this final chapter, I will make the case for a new approach to the CJS. This can be applied across groups but is of particular relevance to those experiencing mental health problems. The most important theme of this book is the devastating impact of the expansion of the penal state and the failure to provide adequately resourced community care services for those experiencing mental health problems. At the time of writing there is some evidence that the tide is turning against both of these policies. While I may, of course, be too optimistic here, I conclude that there is a solution to these problems. It requires a shift so that the CJS is based on a recognition of the fundamental human dignity of all those involved. First though, we need to review how we have reached this position.

Where are we now?

Cavadino and Dignan (2001) coined the term 'punitive managerialism' to describe the shifts that had occurred within UK penal policy outlined above. As Gregory (2007) explains, in the face of persistently high crime rates, official research has shifted from the social causes of crime to an emphasis on crime prevention and the management of individual offenders. Beckett and Western (2001) argue that wider social policy is inextricably linked with developments in penal policy. In their model of analysis, political cultures that emphasise social causes of marginality and offending are much more likely to have a penal policy based on integration, with the result being lower rates of imprisonment. At the other end of this continuum, cultures which conceptualise social problems largely as the result of individual failings lead to penal policies with harsher views on crime – and thus higher rates of imprisonment.

Wilkinson (2000) concludes that a culture, such as the USA, where competitive individualism is a deeply embedded cultural trope will see offenders as unreformable. Tonry (1999) argues that the more inclusive cultures provide a protection against the sorts of moral panics that occur in response to individual high profile crimes or offending. For example, Green (2008) contrasts the media and legal responses to two cases of child murder by children. The murder of James Bulger by two 10-year-old boys in England is consistently constructed as symptomatic of a wider and deep-seated moral decline. On the other hand, the murder of Silje Redergård in Trondheim, Norway, was seen as a tragic one-off and where the perpetrators required expert ongoing intervention with the ultimate aim of their reintegration into society.

The expansion of the penal state

The USA has led the way in the expansion of the use of imprisonment, resulting in a huge prison industrial complex that marginalises even further the most disadvantaged urban communities – particularly African-American ones (Drucker, 2011; Garland, 2001; Gottschalk, 2006; Mauer, 2006; Wacquant, 2009b; Alexander, 2012). What Simon (2014a) has termed the 'arc of punitiveness' began in the mid-1970s driven by a populist response to increases in violent crime and the politicisation of the law and order debate (Simon, 2007). The USA is an outlier in this field, but the use of imprisonment has increased across Europe with England and Wales most closely following the US trends. Nelken (2006) cautions against using Garland's (2001) notion of a 'culture of control' in a simplistic or reductionist fashion, arguing that there are multiple cultures of control. However, it is clear that within these cultures, the general shifts from seeing the CJS as a site of possible social work intervention to viewing it as a risk management processing system are well established. The CJS – once an area of key interest for social work – seems to have been marginalised.

Advise, assist, befriend – and risk manage?

The Probation Act (1907) established that it was a probation officer's role to 'advise, assist and befriend'. In order to practise as a probation officer in the mid-1980s, I had to complete the Certificate of Qualification in Social Work. I undertook placements in CJS settings but, apart from that, the curriculum was essentially the same as my social work colleagues.

The recent history of the probation service in England and Wales reflects the decline of the belief in rehabilitation and reform (Garland 2001). It has moved from a 'social work agency in the CJS', focusing on tackling the social problems that were seen as being the root cause of offending, to a risk-management agency. These reforms, with the introduction of Community Rehabilitation Companies (CRCs), almost totally sever the link between probation and its social work roots. These CRCs will supervise 160,000 offenders who are deemed to be a medium to low risk. The National Probation Service will retain responsibility for high-risk offenders. The economics are fairly clear here: contracts for the supervision of low-risk offenders are much more attractive to companies as the costs will be lower. A Public Accounts Committee report by MPs concludes that the timetable for the introduction of these complex changes has not allowed for the new arrangements to be fully piloted. These reforms follow a pattern of other welfare reforms, where private companies have been given large contracts to deliver services.

In the UK, a key factor for the changes was the decision in 1997 to introduce a new Diploma in Probation Studies (Gregory, 2007). Under the new Diploma, probation officers no longer trained with social work students. As Gregory (2010) notes, the term 'probation officer' was subsequently replaced by a new one – 'offender manager' – a term that almost sums up the decline of the rehabilitative ideal and its replacement by a form of actuarial risk management. In academia, it has become more difficult to find discussions of the impact of mass imprisonment in social work literature. For example, neither the *European Journal of Social Work* nor the *British Journal of Social Work* has published an article in this field in the past year which has specifically addressed the impact of imprisonment on individuals or communities. The focus of social work debate has been on children and families. However, there is a major issue of social justice with significant implications for the most disadvantaged communities in society and it is an issue that social work needs to address.

Stuart Hall and the notion of conjuncture

I approach this discussion having been strongly influenced by Stuart Hall's revival, from Marx and Gramsci, of the term 'conjuncture' – which is simply a combination of events. However, Hall uses it as a tool for the analysis of the current political and cultural trends. Hall was seeking to move away from the rigid economic determinism of Marxism and argues that it is important to consider cultural developments. An economic analysis, Hall suggests, only takes one so far (Cummins, 2014). Using Hall's approach forces us to look at economic and cultural factors.

The potential for reform: the economic case

I am writing this chapter as the 2015 election campaign is entering full swing. It is clear that the issues of taxation and public spending will be at the forefront of the campaign. The CJS has come under increasing scrutiny and there is an irony that the expansion of imprisonment, which has occurred under governments allegedly committed to a small State and fiscal responsibility, might collapse because of the costs. There is a very clear argument that can be made that imprisonment fails on its own terms. This failure is expensive not just in social terms but also financial ones. The National Audit Office study, *Managing Offenders on Short Custodial Sentences* (www.nao.org.uk/report/managing-offenders-on-short-custodial-sentences/), calculated in 2010 that re-offending by ex-offenders in 2007–08 cost the economy between £9.5 and £13 billion – with the vast majority due to offenders who had served short sentences. Meanwhile, the Ministry of Justice's 2013 re-offending statistics show that those on community sentences re-offended significantly less than those given custodial terms. As the Ministry of Justice calculates, the average prison place costs £37,648 per year – around 12 times that of the average probation or community service order.

The Care Act (2014)

The introduction of the Care Act (2014) in England in April 2015 could prove to be a turning point. Similar legislation comes into effect in Wales in April 2016. The new legislation makes it clear where the responsibility lies for the assessment and provision of services to meet the social care needs of prisoners. All adults in prisons or approved premises will be treated as residents of that local authority for the purposes of the Care Act as long as they are in that establishment. This is a very significant change and will have its most profound impact on those local authorities that have a prison within their area. It clearly has a potential impact on all local authorities: if one of their residents is imprisoned and sent to a prison outside of their area, then the duties under the Care Act will move to another authority. For the purposes of the Act, prisoners, as well as adults in prison, include:

- 18 year olds who are in young offender institutions;
- those living in approved premises;
- people who have been required to move from their usual residence as a condition of bail.

Provisions of the Care Act

The provisions of the Care Act apply to all adults. Adults who are in prison and appear to have care and support needs should have these assessed by local authorities. If they meet eligibility criteria, then services should be provided by the authority. This is potentially a very significant group of prisoners. Funding has been provided to individual councils on estimated numbers of prisoners. It has been assumed that the majority of those who will be assessed and may be eligible for support will be older prisoners – that is, those over 50. Prisoners over 60 are the fastest growing group in jail, so there is the potential that there will be a need for increased funding. At the time of writing, this is very much a new policy landscape. It is generally expected that local authorities will work with commissioners of existing prison health care to develop service provision. The politics of this will be interesting; the provision of resources to prisoners will always face some hostility, and this is likely to rise as the pressure on budgets increases.

There are exceptions to the wider provisions of the Care Act that apply to prisoners:

- Prisoners cannot receive direct payments – other choices will be more limited.
- Investigating safeguarding incidents will not be the responsibility of adult social care departments.
- Prisoners will only be able to express preferences for accommodation provided after release.
- Local authorities will not have to protect prisoners' property.

The potential for reform: changing social and cultural attitudes

Taylor (2003) argues that common sense or widely held views are 'not expressed in theoretical terms' – rather, they are spread by images, stories and myths. In this context, the expansion of the CJS has been driven by often racialised images of marginalised groups. However, there is the scope and potential for challenging these attitudes. The 'war on drugs' has clearly been a key factor in the greater use of imprisonment. Fighting a war requires and creates a demonised enemy, and this becomes much harder to sustain if social attitudes to drugs change. The war on drugs – that is, a harsh, punitive response to those involved in any way with using or dealing illegal narcotics – is now widely accepted to be a failure (Gray, 2001; Levy-Pounds, 2010). The Drug Policy Alliance's (2011) analysis of media reporting shows that this failure has been acknowledged around the world. The appeal of harm-reduction strategies and a response to substance misuse that is informed by public health principles will have an inevitable impact on reducing prison numbers. A shift, which sees drug use as essentially an issue of health, will lead to a more social welfare-based response. This is an example of the creation of a space where social workers can have a broader role alongside service users and community groups, and where other professionals can come together to challenge the dominant discourse of punishment.

The potential for reform: changing prison conditions

As noted above, the USA has been the leader of the penal arms race with a huge growth in the prison population over the past 30 years. Simon (2014a) has compared this expansion to a biblical flood. It is a flood that has left a trail of destruction across poor, urban communities, particularly African-American ones. The USA stands apart from other democratic countries in the use of imprisonment. However, England and Wales have been two of its closest European followers. The US rate has stabilised and is now beginning to show signs of falling, and one can discern similar trends in this country. One of the factors has been concerted campaigns, including legal cases about prison conditions – particularly about the provision of health care, which also covers mental health care.

Learning lessons from the USA: *Brown v Plata*

In *Brown v Plata* a group of prisoners successfully sued the State of California, arguing that the State's penal policies, the overcrowding that they produced and the resultant inadequate health care amounted to a breach of the Eighth Amendment's constitutional prohibition of cruel and unusual punishment. Similarly, the Trenčín Statement (WHO, 2007), which outlines the UN position on the treatment of prisoners, states that: 'Prisoners shall have access to the health services available in the country without discrimination on the grounds of their legal situation' (www.euro.who.int/__data/assets/pdf_file/0006/99006/E91402.pdf).

As noted above, the health care needs of prisoners are far greater than those of the wider community, and these are exacerbated by imprisonment. The inevitable result of imprisoning more people for longer was the collapse of a prison health care system. There are echoes of these issues in the most recent report from HM Chief Inspector of Prisons in England and Wales, who highlighted overcrowding and a reduction in the food budget from £2.20 to £1.96 in 2013 as having a significant impact on the worsening conditions in prison.

Justice Kennedy, who wrote the majority decision in *Brown v Plata*, was so appalled by the conditions that existed that he included photographs in the Supreme Court Judgment (see www.supremecourt.gov/opinions/10pdf/09-1233.pdf). These include scenes of chronic overcrowding and 'dry cells' – essentially cages used as holding cells for people waiting for transfer to mental health facilities (see Figures 6.1 and 6.2).

Figure 6.1 *Overcrowding in a California prison*

Figure 6.2 *'Dry cells'*

Garland (2001) argues that the post-war penal system was the 'habitus of the rehabilitative ideal' (p 5), while Wacquant (2008; 2009a; 2009b) argues that the growth of social insecurity and the expansion of the penal state are endogenous features of the neo-liberal political project. The key premises of neo-liberalism have been accepted by parties of both the left and the right. Wacquant identifies that the 'doxa' of the penal state, such as 'prison works', 'zero tolerance' and 'broken windows', have been widely accepted in an uncritical fashion. The 'decline of the rehabilitative ideal' (Garland, 2001) has been one of the most significant shifts in social attitudes in this area over the past 30 years. However, we are now at a point where the tensions and contradictions within these policies create the potential for change.

Conclusion

As noted previously, Seddon (2007) has argued that it is an illusion to think that there is a clear divide between mental health systems and the CJS. There is always an overlap between the two. In particular, there will be specific groups or individuals who present challenges to both systems or who might be placed in either. However, the decline of welfare-based approaches has led to a situation where the CJS has historically been a key site or element of social work intervention. This is a situation that social workers have to challenge. As we have seen throughout this book, there is scope at every stage of the CJS for a less punitive option to be followed, on the basis that the root cause of the individuals' difficulties lies in their mental health. For these options to be taken on a consistent basis, the progressive vision of community care – a properly funded range of mental health services for citizens in need or crisis – needs to be rekindled. This can only be done if we rediscover and recognise the inherent dignity of all in society. This view is best summed up by Justice Kennedy in his decision for the prisoners in *Brown v Plata*:

> ... *prisoners retain the essence of human dignity ... A prison that deprives prisoners of basic sustenance, including adequate medical care, is incompatible with the concept of human dignity and has no place in a civilized society.*

There should be nothing incompatible in the CJS and the mental health system with these principles. As this book sets out to demonstrate, there is much in the CJS that would not pass Justice Kennedy's test. The role of social work and social workers is to ensure that such examples are removed as soon as possible.

Taking it further

Alexander, M (2012) *The New Jim Crow: Mass Incarceration in the Age of Colorblindness*. New York: New Press.

Cavadino, M and Dignan, J (2001) *The Penal System: An Introduction*. London: Sage.

Drucker, E (2011) *A Plague of Prisons: The Epidemiology of Mass Incarceration in America*. New York: New Press.

Harcourt, B (2011) *The Illusion of Free Markets: Punishment and the Myth of Natural Order*. Cambridge, MA: Harvard University Press.

Simon, J (2014) *Mass Incarceration on Trial*. New Press: New York.

Squires, P and Lea, J (eds) (2013) *Criminalisation and Advanced Marginality: Critically Exploring the Work of Loic Wacquant*. Bristol: Policy Press.

United States Supreme Court (2010) Judgment in *Brown v Plata* [online]. Available at: www.supreme-court.gov/opinions/10pdf/09-1233.pdf (accessed 15 December 2015).

Wacquant, L (2009) *Prisons of Poverty*. Minneapolis: University of Minnesota Press.

WHO (2007) Trenčín Statement on Prisons and Mental Health [online]. Available at: www.euro.who.int/__data/assets/pdf_file/0006/99006/E91402.pdf (accessed 15 December 2015).

Bibliography

Aboleda-Florez, J and Holley, H L (1998) Criminalization of the Mentally III: Part II. Initial Detention, *Canadian Journal of Psychiatry*, 33: 87–95.

ACPO/National Centre for Policing Excellence (2006) *Guidance on the Safer Detention and Handling of Persons in Police Custody*. London: ACPO.

Alexander, J G, de Chesnay, M, Marshall, E, Campbell, A R, Johnson, S and Wright, R (1989) Parallel Reactions in Rape Victims and Rape Researchers. *Violence and Victims*, 4(1): 57–62.

Alexander, M (2012) *The New Jim Crow: Mass Incarceration in the Age of Colorblindness*. New York: New Press.

Appleby, L (2010) *Offender Health Reform is Gathering Pace. In Prison Mental Health: Vision and Reality*. London: Centre for Mental Health.

Audit Commission (1994) *Finding A Place: A Review of Mental Health Services for Adults*. London: HMSO.

Barr, H (2001) Policing Madness: People with Mental Illness and the NYPD, in McArdle, A and Erzen, T (eds), *Quality of Life and the New Police Brutality in New York City*. New York: NYU Press.

Bartlett, P and Sandland, R (2003) *Mental Law Policy and Practice* (2nd edition). Oxford: Oxford University Press.

Bartlett, A, Somers, N, Flander, M and Harty, M (2012) *Women Mentally Disordered Offenders: Pathways of Care* (London and Regional Reports). London Secure Commissioning Group.

Bartlett, A, Somers, N, Reeves, C and White, S (2012) Women Prisoners: An Analysis of the Process of Hospital Transfers. *The Journal of Forensic Psychiatry & Psychology*, 23(4): 538–53.

Bartlett, A, Somers, N, Flander, M and Harty, M (2014) Pathways of Care of Women in Secure Hospitals: Which Women go Where and Why? *British Journal of Psychiatry*. London: Royal College of Psychiatrists.

Barton, W R (1959) *Institutional Neurosis*. Bristol: Wright and Sons.

Bauman, Z (1997) *Postmodernity and Its Discontents*. New York: New York University Press.

Bauman, Z (2003) *Wasted Lives: Modernity and Its Outcasts*. Oxford: Polity.

Bauman, Z (2007) *Liquid Times: Living in an Age of Uncertainty*. Oxford: Polity.

Bean, P and Nemitz, T (1994) The Use of the 'Appropriate Adult' Scheme (A Preliminary Report). *Medicine, Science and the Law*, 34(2): 161–6.

Beck, U (1992) *Risk Society: Towards a New Modernity* (translated from the German by Ritter, M). London: Sage.

Beckett, K and Western, B (2001) Governing Social Marginality, in Garland, D (ed) *Mass Imprisonment Social Causes and Consequences*. London: Sage, 35–50.

Beynon, J (1983) Ways-in and Staying-in: Fieldwork as Problem Solving, in Hammersley, M (ed) *The Ethnography of Schooling: Methodological Issues*. Driffield, UK: Nafferton, 37–55.

Bhui, K, Stansfield, S, Hull, S, Priebe, S, Mole, F and Feder, G (2003) Ethnic Variations in Pathways to and Use of Specialist Mental Health Services in the UK. *The British Journal of Psychiatry*, 182(2): 105–16.

Bittner, E (1967a) Police Discretion in Emergency Apprehension of Mentally III Persons. *Social Problems*, 14: 278–92.

Bittner, E (1967b) The Police on Skid Row: A Study of Peace Keeping. *American Sociological Review*, 32(5): 699–715.

Bittner, E (1970) *Functions of the Police in Modern Society*. Washington, DC: NIMH.

Bland, J, Mezey, G and Dolan, B (1999) Special Women, Special Needs: A Descriptive Study of Female Special Hospital Patients. *The Journal of Forensic Psychiatry*, 10(1): 34–45.

Blom-Cooper, L, Hally, H and Murphy, E (1995) *The Falling Shadow: One Patient's Mental Health Care 1978–1993*. London: Duckworth.

Booth, T and Booth, W (1994) The Use of Depth Interviewing with Vulnerable Subjects. *Social Science and Medicine*, 39(3): 415–24.

Borum, R (2000) Improving High Risk Encounters Between People with Mental Illness and the Police. *Journal of the American Academy of Psychiatry and the Law*, 28(3): 332–37.

Borzecki, M and Wormith, J S (1985) The Criminalization of Psychiatrically Ill People: A Review with a Canadian Perspective. *Psychiatric Journal of the University of Ottawa*, 10(4): 241–47.

Bourdieu, P (1998) The Left Hand and the Right Hand of the State, in Bourdieu, P, *Acts of Resistance*. Cambridge: Polity, 1–10.

Brannen, J (1993) The Effects of Research on Participants: The Findings from a Study of Mothers and Employment. *The Sociological Review*, 41(2): 328–46.

British Academy (2014) A Presumption Against Imprisonment [online]. Available at: www.britac.uk (accessed 15 December 2015).

Brown, B, Birtwhistle, J, Roe, L and Thompson, C (1999) The Unhealthy Lifestyle of People with Schizophrenia. *Psychological Medicine*, 29(3): 679–701.

Brown, D, Ellis, T and Larcombe, K (1992) *Changing the Code: Police Detention under the Revised PACE Codes of Practice*. London: HMSO.

Brown, S, Burkhart, B R, King, G D and Solomon, R (1977) Roles and Expectations for Mental Health Professionals in Law Enforcement Agencies. *American Journal of Community Psychology*, 5(2): 207–15.

Browne, D (2009) Black Communities, Mental Health and the Criminal Justice System, in Reynolds, J, Muston, R, Heller, T, Leach, J, McCormick, M, Wallcraft, J and Walsh, M (eds), *Mental Health Still Matters*. Basingstoke: Palgrave MacMillan.

Bryman, A (2012) *Social Research Methods* (4th edition). Oxford: Oxford University Press.

Burr, V (2003) *An Introduction to Social Constructionism* (2nd edition). London: Routledge.

Bushe, G R (1995) Advances in Appreciative Inquiry as an Organization Development Intervention. *Organization Development Journal*, 13(3): 14–22.

Butler, I and Drakeford, M (2001) Which Blair Project? Communitarianism, Social Authoritarianism and Social Work *Journal of Social Work*, 1(1): 7–19.

Care Service Improvement Partnership/Shift (2006) *Mind over Matter: Improving Media Reporting of Mental Health*. London: Sainsbury Centre for Mental Health.

Carey, S J (2001) Police Officers' Knowledge of, and Attitudes to, Mental Illness in Southwest Scotland. *Scottish Medical Journal*, 46(2): 41–2.

Carson, E and Golinelli, D (2013) Prisoners in 2012: Trends in Admissions and Releases 1991–2013 [online]. Available at: www.bjs.gov/content/pub/pdf/p12tar9112.pdf (accessed 15 December 2015).

Cavadino, M and Dignan, J (with others) (2006) *Penal Systems: A Comparative Approach*. London: Sage Publications.

Chan, J (1996) Changing Police Culture. *British Journal of Criminology*, 36(1): 109–34.

Chin, A L (1998) Future Visions: The Unpublished Papers of Abraham Maslow. *Journal of Organizational Change Management*, 11(1): 74–7.

Choongh, S (1997) *Policing as Social Discipline*. Oxford: Clarendon Press.

Clare, I and Gudjonsson, G (1992) *Devising and Piloting an Experimental Version of the 'Notice to Detained Persons'*. London: Royal Commission on Criminal Justice (available from British Library Document Supply Centre, DSC:OP-RC/1099).

Clear, T (2009) *Imprisoning Communities: How Mass Incarceration Makes Disadvantaged Neighborhoods Worse*. New York: Oxford University Press.

Cohen, S (1972) *Folk Devils and Moral Panics*. London: MacGibbon and Kee.

Cooperrider, D L and Srivastva, S (1987) Appreciative Inquiry in Organizational Life. *Research Organizational Change and Development*, 1: 129–69.

Cope, R (1989) The Compulsory Detention of Afro-Caribbeans under the Mental Health Act. *New Community*, 15(3): 343–56.

Corston, J (Chair) (2007) A Report by Baroness Jean Corston of a Review of Women with Particular Vulnerabilities in the Criminal Justice System [online]. Available at: www.justice.gov.uk/publications/docs/corston-report-march-2007.pdf (accessed 15 December 2015).

Cross, S (2010) *Mediating Madness, Mental Distress and Cultural Representation*. Basingstoke: Palgrave Macmillan.

Cummins, I (2006) A Path not Taken? Mentally Disordered Offenders and the Criminal Justice System. *Journal of Social Welfare and Family Law*, 28(3): 267–81.

Cummins, I (2007) Boats Against the Current: Vulnerable Adults in Police Custody. *The Journal of Adult Protection*, 9(1): 15–24.

Cummins, I (2008) A Place of Safety? Self-harming Behaviour in Police Custody. *The Journal of Adult Protection*, 10(1): 36–47.

Cummins, I (2010) Distant Voices, Still Lives: Reflections on the Impact of Media Reporting of the Cases of Christopher Clunis and Ben Silcock. *Ethnicity and Inequalities in Health and Social Care*, 3(4): 18–29.

Cummins, I (2011) The Other Side of Silence: The Role of the Appropriate Adult Post-Bradley. *The Journal of Ethics and Social Welfare*, 5(3): 306–12.

Cummins, I (2011) Deinstitutionalisation: Mental Health Services in the Age of Neo-liberalism. *Social Policy and Social Work in Transition*, 1(2): 55–74.

Cummins, I (2012) Mental Health and Custody: A Follow On Study. *The Journal of Adult Protection*, 14(2): 73–81.

Cummins, I (2013) Policing and Mental Illness in the Era of Deinstitutionalisation and Mass Incarceration: A UK Perspective. *International Journal of Criminology and Sociological Theory*, 6(4): 92–104.

Cummins, I (2013) Using Simon's 'Governing Through Crime' to Explore the Development of Mental Health Policy in England and Wales Since 1983. *Journal of Social Welfare and Family Law*, 34(3): 325–37.

Cummins, I (2014) The Stuart Hall Project. *European Group for the Study of Deviance and Social Control Newsletter* [online]. Available at: www.europeangroup.org/?q=node/61 (accessed 15 December 2015).

Cummins, I (2015) Discussing Race, Racism and Mental Health: Two Mental Health Inquiries Reconsidered. *International Journal of Human Rights in Healthcare*, 8(3): 160–72.

Cummins, I (2015) Reading Wacquant: Social Work and Advanced Marginality. *European Journal of Social Work*, DOI: 10. 1080/13691457.2015.1022861.

Cummins, I and Jones, S (2010) Blue Remembered Skills: Mental Health Awareness Training for Police Officers. *Journal of Adult Protection*, 12(3): 14–19.

Curran, M (1991) Appreciative Inquiry: A Third Wave Approach to OD. *Vision/Action,* December: 12–14.

Curran, S and Matthews, K (2001) The Psychiatrist Will be With You in a Day or Two. Unnecessary Delays in Assessing the Mentally Ill in Police Custody in Scotland. *Scottish Medical Journal*, 46(2): 37.

Davis, M (1998) *City of Quartz: Excavating the Future in Los Angeles*. London: Verso.

Deane, M W, Steadman, H J, Borum, R, Veysey, B M and Morrissey, J P (1999) Emerging Partnerships Between Mental Health and Law Enforcement. *Psychiatric Services*, 50(1): 99–101.

Denzin, N K and Lincoln, Y S (eds) (1994) *Handbook of Qualitative Research*. London: Sage.

Department of Health (1983) *Mental Health Act*. London: HMSO.

Department of Health (1998) *Modernising Mental Health Services: Sound, Safe and Supportive*. London: TSO.

DHSS (1988) *Report of the Committee of Inquiry into the Care and Aftercare of Sharon Campbell* (Chair: J Spokes). London: HMSO.

Downes, D and Hansen, K (2006) Welfare and Punishment [online]. Available at: www.crimeandsociety.org.uk (accessed 15 December 2015).

Drake, C and Cayton, H (1993) *Black Metropolis: A Study of Negro Life in a Northern City*. Chicago: University of Chicago Press.

Drucker, E (2011) *A Plague of Prisons: The Epidemiology of Mass Incarceration in America*. New York: New Press.

Drug Policy Alliance (2011) Drug Policy Alliance and Global Commission on Drug Policy June 2011 Media Report [online]. Available at: www.drugpolicy.org (accessed 15 December 2015).

Duggan, S and Rutherford, M (2007) *Forensic Mental Health Services Facts and Figures on Current Provision*. London: Sainsbury Centre for Mental Health.

Dunn, J and Fahy, T A (1987) Section 136 and the Police. *Bulletin of the Royal College of Psychiatry*, 11: 224–5.

Eastman, N and Starling, B (2006) Mental Disorder Ethics: Theory and Empirical Investigation. *Journal of Medical Ethics,* 32(2): 94–9.

Eaton, W W (1980) *The Sociology of Mental Disorders.* New York: Praeger.

Etherington, K (1996) The Counsellor as Researcher: Boundary Issues and Critical Dilemmas. *British Journal of Guidance and Counselling,* 24(3): 339–46.

Fallon, P, Blueglass, R, Edwards, B and Daniels, G (1999) *Report of the Committee of Inquiry into the Personality Disorder Unit, Ashworth Special Hospital (CM 4195).* London: HMSO.

Fazel, S and Benning, R (2009) Suicides in Female Prisoners in England and Wales, 1978–2004. *The British Journal of Psychiatry,* 194(2): 183–4.

Feeley, M and Simon, J (1994) Actuarial Justice: The emerging New Criminal Law, in Nelken, D (ed), *The Futures of Criminology.* London: Sage, 173–201.

Fennell, P (1994) Mentally Disordered Suspects in the Criminal Justice System. *Journal of Law and Society,* 21(1): 57–71.

Fernando, S (1988) *Race and Culture in Psychiatry.* London: Routledge.

Fernando, S, Ndegwa, D and Wilson, M (1998) *Forensic Psychiatry, Race and Culture.* London: Routledge.

Fisher, Sir H (1977) *Report of an Inquiry by the Hon. Sir Henry Fisher into the Circumstances Leading to the Trial of Three Persons on Charges Arising Out of the Death of Maxwell Confait and the Fire at 27 Doggett Road, London SE6.* London: HMSO.

Ford, R, Duncan, G, Warner, L, Hardy, P and Mien, M (1998) One Day Survey by the Mental Health Act Commission of Acute Adult Psychiatric In-patient Wards in England and Wales. *British Medical Journal,* 317(7168): 1279–83.

Foucault, M (1972) *The Archaeology of Knowledge* (translation Sheridan-Smith, A M). London: Tavistock.

Foucault, M (1982) The Subject and Power, in Hubert, L D and Rabinow, P, *Michel Foucault: Beyond Structuralism and Hermeneutics.* Brighton: Harvester Press.

Foucault, M (1991) *Discipline and Punish: The Birth of the Prison* (translation Sheridan, A). London: Penguin.

Foucault, M (2001) *Madness and Civilisation* (translation Howard, R) New York: Vintage.

Foucault, M (2003) *The Birth of the Clinic.* Abingdon: Routledge.

Foucault, M (2006) *The History of Madness.* Abingdon: Routledge.

Foucault, M (2008) *The Birth of Biopolitics: Lectures at the Collège de France, 1978–1979* (translation Burchell, G). Basingstoke: Palgrave.

Fry, A J, O'Riordan, D P and Geanelos, R (2002) Social Control Agents or Frontline Carers for People with Mental Health Problems: Police and Mental Health. *Health & Social Care in the Community,* 10(4): 277–86.

Furedi, F (1994) A Plague of Moral Panics. *Living Marxism,* 73 (November): 20.

Gale, T, Hawley, C and Sivakumaran, T (2003) Do Mental Health Professionals Really Understand Probability? Implications for Risk Assessment and Evidence-based Practice. *Journal of Mental Health,* 12(4): 417–30.

Gardner, A (2011) *Personalisation in Social Work.* Exeter: Learning Matters.

Garfinkel, H (1967) *Studies in Ethnomethodology.* Englewood Cliffs, NJ: Prentice-Hall.

Garland, D (2001) *The Culture of Control: Crime and Social Order in Contemporary Society.* Chicago: University of Chicago Press.

Garland, D (2004) Beyond the Culture of Control. *Critical Review of International Social and Political Philosophy* (Special issue on Garland's *The Culture of Control*), 7(2): 160–89.

Garrett, P (2013) *Social Work and Social Theory: Making Connections.* Bristol: Policy Press.

Garrett, P M (2007) Making Social Work More Bourdieusian: Why the Social Work Profession Should Engage with the Work of Pierre Bourdieu. *European Journal of Social Work,* 10(2): 225–43.

Gelsthorpe, L (2010) Women, Crime and Control: Criminal Justice. *Criminology and Criminal Justice,* 10(4): 375–86.

Gergen, K (1994) *Realities and Relationships: Soundings in Social Construction.* Cambridge, MA: Harvard University Press.

Giddens, A (1991) *The Consequences of Modernity.* Cambridge: Polity Press.

Giddens, A (1998) *The Third Way: The Renewal of Social Democracy.* Oxford: Blackwell.

Gillig, P M, Dumaine, M, Stammer, J W, Hillard, J R and Grubb, P (1990) What do Police Officers Really Want from the Mental Health System. *Hospital and Community Psychiatry,* 41(6): 663–5.

Gilmour, I (1992) *Dancing with Dogma: Britain under Thatcherism.* London: Simon and Schuster.

Gilroy, P (2002) *There Ain't No Black in the Union Jack*. London: Routledge.

Giroux, H (2011) Neoliberalism and the Death of the Social State: Remembering Walter Benjamin's Angel of History Social Identities. *Journal for the Study of Race, Nation and Culture*, 17(4): 587–601.

Gittins, D (1998) *Madness in its Place: Narratives of Severalls Hospital 1913–1997*. London: Routledge.

Goffman, E (1961) *Asylums: Essays on the Social Situation of Mental Patients and Other Inmates*. Harmondsworth: Penguin.

Goldberg, D and Huxley, P (1980) *Mental Illness in the Community*. London: Tavistock.

Goldsmith, A (1990) Taking Police Culture Seriously: Police Discretion and the Limits of Law. *Policing and Society*, 1(2): 91–114.

Gostin, L (2007) From a Civil Libertarian to a Sanitarian. *Journal of Law and Society*, 34(4): 594–616.

Gottschalk, M (2006) *The Prison and the Gallows: The Politics of Mass Incarceration in America*. Cambridge: Cambridge University Press.

Graham, J (2001) Policing and the Mentally Disordered. *Scottish Medical Journal*, 46(2): 38–9.

Gramsci, A (1971) *Selections from the Prison Notebooks*. London: Lawrence and Wishart.

Grant, S and Humphries, M (2006) Critical Evaluation of Appreciative Inquiry: Bridging an Apparent Paradox. *Action Research*, 4(4): 401–18.

Gray, J P (2001) *Why Our Drug Laws have Failed and What Can We do About It: A Judicial Indictment of the War on Drugs*. Philadelphia: Temple University Press.

Green, D A (2008) *When Children Kill Children: Penal Populism and Political Culture*. Oxford: Oxford University Press.

Gregory, M (2007) Newly Qualified Probation Officers Talk About Their Training. *Social Work Education*, 26(1): 53–68.

Gregory, M (2010) Reflection and Resistance: Probation Practice and the Ethic of Care. *British Journal of Social Work*, 40(4): 2274–90.

Gripsrud, J (2002) *Understanding Media Culture*. London: Arnold.

Gudjonsson, G and MacKeith, J (1997) *Disputed Confessions and the Criminal Justice System (Maudsley Discussion Paper No. 2)*. London: Institute of Psychiatry.

Habermas, J (1976) *Legitimation Crisis*. London: Heinemann.

Haley, M and Swift, J A (1988) PACE and the Social Worker: A Step in the Right Direction? The *Journal of Social Welfare Law*, 10(6): 355–73.

Hall, S (ed) (1997) *Representation: Cultural Representations and Signifying Practices*. London: Routledge.

Hall, S, Critcher, C, Jefferson, T, Clarke, J and Roberts, B (2013) *Policing the Crisis: Mugging, the State and Law and Order* (35th anniversary edition). Basingstoke: Palgrave Macmillan.

Hallam, A (2002) Media Influences on Mental Health Policy: Long-term Effects of the Clunis and Silcock Cases. *International Review of Psychiatry*, 14(1): 26–33.

Hallsworth, S and Lea, J (2011) Reconstructing Leviathan: Emerging Contours of the Security State. *Theoretical Criminology*, 15(2), 141–57.

Harcourt, B (2011) *The Illusion of Free Markets: Punishment and the Myth of Natural Order*. Cambridge, MA: Harvard University Press.

Hartford, K, Heslop, L, Stitt, L and Hoch, J (2005) Design of an Algorithm to Identify Persons with Mental Illness in a Police Administrative Database. *International Journal of Law and Psychiatry*, 28(1): 1–11.

Heginbotham, C, Hale, R, Warren, L, Walsh, T and Carr, J (1994) *The Report of the Independent Panel of Inquiry Examining the Case of Michael Buchanan*. London: London Mental Health Trust.

Herbert, S K (1997) *Policing Space: Territoriality and the Los Angeles Police Department*. Minneapolis: University of Minnesota Press.

Hindler, C (1999) The Supervision Register: 19 Months After its Introduction. *Psychiatric Bulletin*, 23: 15–19.

HM Chief Inspector of Prisons for England and Wales (2014) *Annual Report 2013–14*. London: HMSO.

HM Government (1983) *Mental Health Act 1983* [online]. Available at: www.legislation.gov.uk/ukpga/1983/20/contents (accessed 15 December 2015).

Holdaway, S (1983) *Inside the British Police*. Oxford: Blackwell.

Holmes-Eber, P and Riger, S (1990) Hospitalisation and Composition of Mental Patients' Social Networks. *Schizophrenia Bulletin*, 16(1): 157–64.

Home Office (1984) *Police and Criminal Evidence Act* [online]. Available at: www.legislation.gov.uk/ukpga/1984/60/contents (accessed 15 December 2015).

Home Office (1990) Provision for Mentally Disordered Offenders. *Circular 66/90.*

Home Office (1995) Mentally Disordered Offenders: Inter-Agency Working. *Circular 12/95.*

Home Office (1995) *Police and Criminal Evidence Act 1984: Codes of Practice.* London: HMSO.

Home Office (2003) *Guidance for Appropriate Adults.* London: HMSO.

Home Office/Cabinet (2002) *PACE Review Report of the Joint Home Office/Cabinet Office Review of the Police and Criminal Evidence Act 1984.* London: HMSO.

Hopton, J (2006) The Future of Critical Psychiatry. *Critical Social Policy*, 26(1): 57–73.

Hough, M (2003) Modernisation and Public Opinion: Some Criminal Justice Paradoxes. *Contemporary Politics*, 9(2): 143–55.

Howard, J (1780) *The State of the Prisons in England and Wales* (2nd edition). Warrington and London: T. Caudal.

Howard League (2010) Voice of a Child [online]. Available at: www.howardleague.org.uk (accessed 15 December 2015).

Hubbard, B M (1998) *Conscious Evolution: Awakening the Power of Our Social Potential.* Novato, CA: New World Library.

Husted, J R, Charter, R A and Perrou, B (1995) California Law Enforcement Agencies and the Mentally Ill Offender. *Bulletin of the American Academy of Psychiatry and Law.* 23(2): 315–29.

Ignatieff, M (1985) State, Civil Society and Total Institutions, in Cohen, S and Scull, A (eds), *Social Control and the State: Historical and Comparative Essays.* Oxford: Blackwell.

Irwin, J (2004) *The Warehouse Prison: Disposal of the New Dangerous Class.* Oxford: Oxford University Press.

Israel, M (2004) Strictly Confidential? Integrity and the Disclosure of Criminological and Socio-legal Research. *British Journal of Criminology*, 44(5): 715–40.

Jackson, J (2004) Experience and Expression: Social and Cultural Significance in the Fear of Crime. *British Journal of Criminology*, 44(6): 946–66.

James, D (2000) Police Station Diversion Schemes: Role and Efficacy in Central London. *Journal of Forensic Psychiatry*, 11(3): 532–55.

Janus, S S, Bess, B E, Cadden, J J and Greenwald, H (1980) Training Police Officers to Distinguish Mental Illness. *American Journal of Psychiatry*, 137(2): 228–9.

Jones, K (1960) *Mental Health and Social Policy 1845–1959.* London: Routledge and Kegan Paul.

Jones, M (2010) The Impedimenta State: Anatomies of Neoliberal Penality. *Criminology and Criminal Justice*, 10(4): 393–404.

Jones, O (2011) *Chavs: The Demonization of the Working Class.* London: Verso.

Jones, S L and Mason, T (2002) Quality of Treatment Following Police Detention of Mentally Disordered Offenders. *Journal of Psychiatric and Mental Health Nursing*, 9(1): 73–80.

Kellner, D (1995) *Media Culture: Cultural Studies, Identity and Politics Between the Modern and the Post Modern.* London: Routledge.

Kelly, B (2005) Structural Violence and Schizophrenia. *Social Science and Medicine*, 61(3): 721–30.

Kelly, B (2007) Penrose's Law in Ireland: An Ecological Analysis of Psychiatric Inpatients and Prisoners. *Irish Medical Journal*, 100(2): 373–4.

Kimhi, R, Barak, Y, Guzman, J, Melamed, Y, Zohar, M and Barak, I (1998) Police Attitudes Toward Mental Illness and Psychiatric Patients in Israel. *Journal of American Academy of Psychiatry and the Law*, 26(4): 625–30.

Knowles, C (2000) *Bedlam on the Streets.* London: Routledge.

Lacey, N (2008) *The Prisoners' Dilemma: Political Economy and Punishment in Contemporary Democracies.* Cambridge: Cambridge University Press.

Laing, R (1959) *The Divided Self.* London: Tavistock.

Laing, R (1967) *The Politics of Experience and the Bird of Paradise.* Harmondsworth: Penguin.

Lamb, H R, Weinberger, L E and DeCuir, W J (2002) The Police and Mental Health. *Psychiatric Services*, 53(10): 1266–71.

Large, M and Nielssen, O (2009) The Penrose Hypothesis in 2004. *Psychology and Psychotherapy: Theory, Research and Practice*, 82(1): 113–19.

Latham, A (1997) The Cinderella Section: Room for Improvement in the Documentation and Implementation of Section 136 of the Mental Health Act 1983. *Journal of Clinical Forensic Medicine*, 4(4): 173–5.

Leff, J and Trieman, N (2000) Long-stay Patients Discharged from Psychiatric Hospital. *British Journal of Psychiatry*, 176(13): 217–23.

Levy-Pounds, N (2010) Can These Bones Live? A Look at the Impacts of the War on Drugs on Poor African-American Children and Families. *Hastings Race & Poverty Law Journal*, 353–80.

Lieberman, J (2015) *Shrinks: The Untold Story of Psychiatry*. London: Wiedenfeld and Nicholson.

Liebling, A, Price, D and Elliott, C (1999) Appreciative Inquiry and Relationships in Prison. *Punishment and Society*, 1(1): 71–98.

Lipkin, R (1990) Free Will, Responsibility and the Promise of Forensic Psychiatry. *International Journal of Law and Psychiatry*, 13(4): 331–58.

Loader, I and Mulcahy, A (2003) *Policing and the Condition of England*. Oxford: Oxford University Press.

Ludema, J D (2002) Appreciative Storytelling: A Narrative Approach to Organization Development and Change, in Fry, R, Barrett, F, Seiling, J and Whitney, D (eds), *Appreciative Inquiry and Organizational Transformation: Reports from the Field*. Westport, CT: Quorum Books.

Lurigio, A (2011) People with Serious Mental Illness in the Criminal Justice System: Causes, Consequences and Correctives. *The Prison Journal* 91(3): 66–86.

Lurigio, A and Watson, A C (2010) The Police and People with Mental Illness: New Approaches to a Longstanding Problem. *Journal of Police Crisis Negotiations*, 10(1–2): 3–14.

Manchester Evening News (25 August 2009) Top Tory Compares Moss Side to The Wire.

Manning, P (3–5 August 1993) Toward a Theory of Police Organization: Polarities and Change. *Paper given to the International Conference on Social Change in Policing*, Taipei.

Marable, M (2011) *Malcolm X: A Life of Reinvention*. London: Allen Lane.

Martin, J P (1985) *Hospitals in Trouble*. Oxford: Blackwell.

Martinson, R (1974) What Works? *The Public Interest*, 34 (Spring).

Mauer, M (2006) *The Race to Incarcerate*. New York: New Press.

McCabe, S, Wallington, P, Alderson, J, Gostin, L and Mason, C (1988) *The Police, Public Order and Civil Liberties*. London: Routledge.

McDonough, J and McDonough, S (1997) *Research Methods for English Language Teachers*. London: Arnold.

McGilloway, S and Donnelly, M (2004) Mental Illness in the UK Criminal Justice System: A Police Liaison Scheme for Mentally Disordered Offenders in Belfast. *Journal of Mental Health*, 13(3): 263–75.

Measor, L (2013) Loic Wacquant, Gender and Cultures of Resistance, in Squires, P and Lea, J (eds), *Criminalisation and Advanced Marginality: Critically Exploring the Work of Loic Wacquant*. Bristol: Policy Press, 129–51.

Meehan, A J (1995) From Conversion to Coercion: The Police Role in Medication Compliance. *Psychiatric Quarterly*, 66(2): 163–84.

Mental Health Foundation (1994) *Creating Community Care: Report of the Mental Health Foundation Inquiry into Community Care for People with Severe Mental Illness*. London: The Mental Health Foundation.

MHAC (2005) *In Place of Fear? The Mental Health Act Commission Eleventh Biennial Report 2003–2005*. London: HMSO.

Michael, S (2005) The Promise of Appreciative Inquiry as an Interview Tool for Field Research. *Development in Practice*, 15(2): 222–30.

MIND (2007) *Another Assault: MIND's Campaign for Equal Access to Justice for People with Mental Health Problems*. London: MIND.

Ministry of Justice (2013) *Transforming Rehabilitation. A Strategy for Reform*. London: TSO.

Moon, G (2000) Risk and Protection: The Discourse of Confinement in Contemporary Mental Health Policy. *Health & Place*, 6(3): 239–50.

Morabito, M (2007) Horizons of Context: Understanding the Police Decision to Arrest People with Mental Illness. *Psychiatric Services* 58(12): 1582–7.

Murphy, E (1991) *After the Asylums: Community Care for People with Mental Illness*. London: Faber and Faber.

Murray, C (1990) *The Emerging British Underclass (Choice in Welfare)*. London: IEA.

Nelken, D (2006) Comparative Criminal Justice: Beyond Ethnocentrism and Relativism. *European Journal of Criminology*, 6(4): 291 311.

Newburn, T and Hayman, S (2002) *Policing, Surveillance and Social Control: CCTV and Police Monitoring of Suspects*. Cullompton: Willan.

Nietzsche, F (1996) *On the Genealogy of Morals: A Polemic by Way of Clarification and Supplement to my Last Book, Beyond Good and Evil* (translated with introduction and notes by Smith, D). Oxford: Oxford University Press.

Nozick, R (1974) *Anarchy, State and Utopia*. New York: Basic Books.

Nye, R (2003) The Evolution of the Concept of Medicalisation in the Twentieth Century. *Journal of the History of Behavioural Sciences*, 39(2): 115–29.

O'Brien, M and Penna, S (1996) Postmodern Theory and Politics: Perspectives on Citizenship and Social Justice. *Innovation: The European Journal of Social Sciences*, 9(2): 185–203.

Office of the Deputy Prime Minister (2004) *Mental Health and Social Exclusion: Social Exclusion Unit Report*. London: HMSO.

Palys, T and Lowman, J (2001) Sociological Research with Eyes Wide Shut: The Limited Confidentiality Dilemma. *Canadian Journal of Criminology*, 43(2): 255–67.

Parton, N (ed) (1996) *Social Work, Risk and the 'Blaming System' in Social Work Theory, Social Change and Social Work*. London: Routledge.

Penrose, L S (1939) Mental Disease and Crime: Outline of a Comparative Study of European Statistics. *British Journal of Medical Psychology,* 18(1): 1–15.

Penrose, L S (1943) A Note on the Statistical Relationship Between Mental Deficiency and Crime in the United States. *American Journal of Mental Deficiency*, 47: 462.

Pierpoint, H (2000) How Appropriate Are Volunteers as 'Appropriate Adults' for Young Suspects? The 'Appropriate Adult' System and Human Rights. *Journal of Social Welfare and Family Law*, 22(4): 383–400.

Pilger, J (1976) Dumped on the Streets and in the Slums: 5000 Who Need Help. *Daily Mirror* [online]. Available at: study more.org.uk/mhhtim.htm (accessed 15 December 2015).

Pilgrim, D and Rogers, A (2013) *Sociology of Mental Health and Illness*. Buckingham: Open University Press.

Pinfold, V, Huxley, P, Thornicroft, G, Farmer, P, Toulmin, H and Graham, T (2003) Reducing Psychiatric Stigma and Discrimination. Evaluating an Educational Intervention with the Police Force in England. *Social Psychiatry and Psychiatric Epidemiology*, 38(6): 337–44.

Pogrebin, M (1986) Police Responses for Mental Health Assistance. *Psychiatric Quarterly* 58(1): 66–73.

Pollitt, C and Bouckaert, G (2003) *Public Management Reform: A Comparative Analysis*. Oxford: Oxford University Press.

Prins, H (Chair) (1993) *Report of the Committee of Inquiry into the Death at Broadmoor Hospital of Orville Blackwood and Review of the Deaths of Two Other Afro-Caribbean Patients. 'Big, Black and Dangerous?'*. London: Special Hospitals Service Authority.

Prospero, M and Kim, M (2009) Ethnic Difference in the Effects of Coercion on Mental Health and the Use of Therapy. *Journal of Social Work Practice*, 23(1): 77–91.

Punch, M (1989) Researching Police Deviance: A Personal Encounter with the Limitations and Liabilities. *British Journal of Sociology*, 40(2): 177–220.

Reason, P (2000) Action Research as Spiritual Practice [online]. Available at: people.bath.ac.uk/mnspwr/Thoughtpieces/ARspiritualpractice.htm (accessed 15 December 2015).

Reiner, R (2000a) Police Research, in King, R D and Wincup, E (eds), *Doing Research on Crime and Justice*. Oxford: Oxford University Press, 205–35.

Reiner, R (2000b) *The Politics of the Police*. Oxford: Oxford University Press.

Riley, G, Freeman, E, Laidlaw, J and Pugh, D (2011) A Frightening Experience: Detainees and Carers' Experiences of Being Detained Under Section 136 of the Mental Health Act. *Medicine, Science and the Law*, 51(3): 164–9.

Ritchie, J (Chair) (1994) *The Report of the Inquiry into the Care and Treatment of Christopher Clunis*. London: HMSO.

Robertson, G, Pearson, R and Gibb, R (1995) *Entry of Mentally Ill People into the Criminal Justice System*. London: Home Office.

Robinson, G, Priede, C, Farrall, S and Shapland, J (2013) Doing 'Strengths Based' Research: Appreciative Inquiry in a Probation Setting. *Criminology and Criminal Justice*, 13(1): 3–20.

Rogers, A (1990) Policing Mental Disorder: Controversies, Myths and Realities. *Social Policy and Administration*, 24(3): 226–37.

Rogers, A and Faulkner, A (1987) *A Place of Safety: MIND's Research into Police Referrals to the Psychiatric Services.* London: MIND.

Rogers, P J and Fraser, D (2003) Appreciating Appreciative Inquiry, in Preskill, H and Coghlan, A T (eds), *Using Appreciative Inquiry in Evaluation.* San Francisco, CA: Jossey-Bass, 75–84.

Rose, D (1998) Television, Madness and Community Care. *Journal of Community and Applied Social Psychology*, 8(3): 213–28.

Rosenhan, D L (1975) On Being Sane in Insane Places. *Science*, 179(4070): 250–8.

Rothman, D (2002) *The Discovery of the Asylum: Social Order and Disorder in the New Republic.* New York: Aldine de Gruyter.

Royal College of Nursing (2004) Health and Nursing Care in the Criminal Justice Service [online]. Available at: www.rcn. org.uk (accessed 15 December 2015).

Royal College of Psychiatrists (RCP) (2008) *Fair Deal for Mental Health: Our Manifesto for a 3 Year Campaign for Tackling Inequality in Mental Healthcare.* London: RCP.

Runciman, Viscount (Chair) (1993) *Royal Commission on Criminal Justice* (Cmnd 22363, Report). London: HMSO.

Sackmann, S (1991) *Cultural Knowledge in Organizations.* Newbury Park, CA: Sage.

Sainsbury Centre for Mental Health (August 2009). *Briefing 39: Mental Health Care and the Criminal Justice System.* London: Sainsbury Centre for Mental Health.

Saunders, P (2005) *The Poverty Wars: Reconnecting Research with Reality.* Sydney: UNSW Press.

Sayce, L (2000) *From Psychiatric Patient to Citizen: Overcoming Discrimination and Social Exclusion.* Basingstoke: Macmillan.

Scott, R D (1973) The Treatment Barrier: Part 1. *British Journal of Medical Psychology*, 46(1): 45–53.

Scull, A (1977) *Decarceration: Community Treatment and the Deviant – A Radical View.* Englewood Cliffs, NJ: Prentice-Hall.

Scull, A (1986) Mental Patients and the Community: A Critical Note. *International Journal of Law and Psychiatry*, 9(3): 383–92.

Scull, A (1989) *Social Order/Mental Disorder: Anglo-American Psychiatry in Historical Perspective.* Berkeley: University of California Press.

Scull, A (2015) *Madness in Civilization: A Cultural History of Insanity.* London: Thames and Hudson.

Secker, J and Harding, C (2002) Users' Perceptions of an African and Caribbean Mental Health Resource Centre. *Health and Social Care in the Community*, 10(4): 270–6.

Seddon, T (2007) *Punishment and Madness.* Abingdon: Routledge-Cavendish.

Sedgwick, P (1982) *Psychopolitics.* London: Pluto Press.

Sharpley, M, Hutchinson, G, McKenzie, K and Murray, R M (2001) Understanding the Excess of Psychosis Among the African-Caribbean Population in England: Review of Current Hypotheses. *British Journal of Psychiatry*, 178(40): 60–8.

Shaw, J, Baker, D, Hunt, I, Moline, A and Appleby, L (2004) Suicide by Prisoners. *British Journal of Psychiatry*, 184(3): 263–7.

Sieff, L (2001) Media Frames of Mental Illness: The Potential Impact of Negative Frames. *Journal of Mental Health*, 12(3): 259–69.

Simon, J (2007) *Governing Through Crime: How the War on Crime Transformed American Democracy and Created a Culture of Fear.* Oxford: Oxford University Press.

Simon, J (2014a) *Mass Incarceration on Trial.* New York: New Press.

Simon, J (2014b) The Cruelty of Abolitionists. *Journal of Human Rights Practice*, 6(3): 486–502.

Simpson, A, Miller, C and Bowers, L (2003) The History of the Care Programme Approach in England: Where Did It Go Wrong? *Journal of Mental Health*, 12(5): 489–504.

Sims, A C and Symonds, R L (1975) Psychiatric Referrals from the Police. *British Journal of Psychiatry*, 127(2): 171–8.

Singleton, N, Meltzer, H and Gatward, R (1998) *Psychiatric Morbidity Among Prisoners in England and Wales.* London: HMSO.

Skinns, L (2011) *Police Custody: Governance, Legitimacy and Reform in the Criminal Justice Process*. Oxford: Willan Publishing.

Skolnick, J (1966) *Justice Without Trial: Law Enforcement in Democratic Society*. New York: Wiley.

Skolnick, J and Fyfe, J (1994) *Above the Law: Police and the Excessive Use of Force*. London: Simon & Schuster.

Slater, T (2009) 'Ghettos' and 'Anti-urbanism' Entries, in Kitchin, R and Thrift, N (eds), *The International Encyclopaedia of Human Geography*. London: Elsevier.

Slater, T (2012) The Myth of 'Broken Britain': Welfare Reform and the Production of Ignorance. *Antipode*, 46(4): 948–69.

Smith, J P (1990) Police are Best at Community Care of Mentally Ill People in England. *Journal of Advanced Nursing*, 15(10): 1117.

Southern Poverty Law Center (2014) Cruel Confinement: Abuse, Discrimination and Death within Alabama's Prisons [online]. Available at: www.splcenter.org (accessed 15 December 2015).

Squires, P and Lea, J (eds) (2013) *Criminalisation and Advanced Marginality: Critically Exploring the Work of Loic Wacquant*. Bristol: Policy Press.

Stake, R E (1995) *The Art of Case Study Research*. Thousand Oaks, CA: Sage.

Staub, M (2014) *Madness is Civilization: When the Diagnosis Was Social, 1948–1980*. London: University of Chicago Press.

Steadman, H J, Deane, M W, Borum, R and Morrissey, J P (2000) Comparing Outcomes of Major Models of Police Responses to Mental Health Emergencies. *Psychiatric Services*, 51(5): 645–9.

Stevenson, C, McDonnell, S, Lennox, C, Shaw, J and Senior, J (2011). Share, Don't Hoard: The Importance of Information Exchange in 21st Century Health–Criminal Justice Partnerships. *Criminal Behaviour and Mental Health*, 21(3): 157–62.

Stone, L (1982) *An Exchange with Michel Foucault*. New York: New York Review of Books.

Subramanian, R and Shames, A (2013) *Sentencing and Prison Practices in Germany and the Netherlands: Implications for the United States*. New York: Vera Institute of Justice.

Szasz, T (1963) *Law, Liberty and Psychiatry*. New York: Macmillan.

Szasz, T (1971) *The Manufacture of Madness*. London: Routledge and Kegan Paul.

Taylor, C (2003) *Modern Social Imaginaries*. Durham, NC: Duke University Press.

Taylor, C and White, S (2000) *Practising Reflexivity in Health and Welfare: Making Knowledge*. Buckingham: Open University Press.

Taylor, P and Gunn, J (1999) Homicides by People with Mental Illness: Myth and Reality. *Journal of Psychiatry*, 174(1): 9–14.

Teplin, L (1984) Criminalising Mental Disorder. *American Psychologist*, 39: 794–803.

Teplin, L A (1985) The Criminality of the Mentally Ill: A Dangerous Misconception. *American Journal of Psychiatry*, 142(5): 593–9.

Tesse, C F and van Wormer, J (1975) Mental Health Training and Consultation with Suburban Police. *Community Mental Health Journal*, 11(2): 115–21.

Tonry, M (1999) Why are US Incarceration Rates so High? *Crime and Delinquency*, 45(4): 419–37.

Tummey, R and Turner, T (2008) *Critical Issues in Mental Health*. Basingstoke: Macmillan.

Turbett, C (2011) Personalisation in Social Work. *British Journal of Social Work*, 41(7): 1406–08.

Tyler, I (2013) *Revolting Subjects, Social Abjection and Resistance in Neoliberal Britain*. London: Zed Books.

US Department of Health and Human Services (1999) *Mental Health: A Report of the Surgeon General*. Rockville, MD: US Department of Health and Human Services.

Vaughan, P J, Kelly, M and Pullen, N (2001) The Working Practices of the Police in Relation to Mentally Disordered Offenders and Diversion Services. *Medicine, Science and the Law*, 41(1): 13–20.

Wacquant, L (2000) The New 'Peculiar Institution': On the Prison as Surrogate Ghetto. *Theoretical Criminology*, 4(3): 377–89 (special issue on *New Social Studies of the Prison*, edited by Bosworth, M and Sparks, R).

Wacquant, L (2002) From Slavery to Mass Incarceration. *New Left Review*, 13: 41–60.

Wacquant, L (2005) Race as Civic Felony. *International Social Science Journal*, 57(183): 127–42.

Wacquant, L (2006) *Body & Soul: Notebooks of an Apprentice Boxer*. Oxford: Oxford University Press.

Wacquant, L. (2006) The Scholarly Myths of the New Law-and-Order Doxa, in Panitch, L and Leys, C (eds), *The Socialist Register 2006: Telling the Truth*. London: Merlin Press/New York: Monthly Review Press, 93–115.

Wacquant, L (2008a) Ghettos and Anti-Ghettos: An Anatomy of the New Urban Poverty. *Thesis Eleven*, 94: 113–18.

Wacquant, L (2008b) *Urban Outcasts: A Comparative Sociology of Advanced Marginality*. Cambridge: Polity Press.

Wacquant, L (2009a) *Punishing the Poor: The Neoliberal Government of Social Insecurity*. Durham, NC: Duke University Press.

Wacquant, L (2009b) *Prisons of Poverty*. Minneapolis: University of Minnesota Press.

Wacquant, L. (2009c) The Body, the Ghetto and the Penal State. *Qualitative Sociology*, 32(1): 101–29.

Wacquant, L (2010) Class, Race and Hyperincarceration in Revanchist America. *Daedalus*, 140(3): 74–90 (Summer thematic issue on *The Challenges of Mass Incarceration*).

Wacquant, L (2010) Crafting the Neoliberal State: Workfare, Prisonfare and Social Insecurity. *Sociological Forum*, 25(2): 197–220 (with responses by Campbell, J, Harcourt, B, Mayer, M, Peck, J, Piven, F and Valverde, M, in *Theoretical Criminology*, 14(1), February 2010).

Wacquant, L (2010) Urban Desolation and Symbolic Denigration in the Hyperghetto. *Social Psychology Quarterly*, 20(2): 1–5.

Wacquant, L (2011) A Janus-Faced Institution of Ethnoracial Closure: A Sociological Specification of the Ghetto, in Hutchison, R and Haynes, B (eds), *The Ghetto: Contemporary Global Issues and Controversies*, Boulder, CO: Westview, 1–31.

Wacquant, L (2012) Probing the Meta-Prison. Preface to Ross, J I (ed), *The Globalization of Supermax Prisons*. New Brunswick: Rutgers University Press.

Wacquant, L (2012) Three Steps to a Historical Anthropology of Actually Existing Neoliberalism. *Social Anthropology*, 19(4) (November): 66–79 (with responses by Bockman, J, Hilgers, M, Peck, J, Brenner, N, Theodore, N and Collier, S).

Waddington, P (1999) Police (Canteen) Sub-culture: An Appreciation. *British Journal of Criminology*, 39(2): 287–309.

Wahl, O (2003) Depictions of Mental Illnesses in Children's Media. *Journal of Mental Health*, 12(3): 249–58.

Walmsley, R (2013) World Female Imprisonment List [online]. Available at: www.prisonstudies.org/sites/prisonstudies.org/files/resources/downloads/wfil_2nd_edition.pdf (accessed 15 December 2015).

Ward, M and Applin, C (1998) *The Unlearned Lesson*. London: Wynne Howard.

Warner, L, Nicholas, S, Patel, K, Harris, J and Ford, R (2000) *National Visit 2: A Visit by the Mental Health Act Commission to 104 Mental Health and Learning Disability Units in England and Wales – Improving Care for Detained Patients from Black and Ethnic Minority Communities*. London: Sainsbury Centre for Mental Health.

Watson, A C, Corrigan, P W and Ottati, V (2004a) Police Officers' Attitudes Toward and Decisions About Persons with Mental Illness. *Psychiatric Services*, 55(1): 49–53.

Watson, A C, Corrigan, P W and Ottati, V (2004b) Police Responses to Persons with Mental Illness: Does the Label Matter? *Journal of the American Academy of Psychiatry and the Law*, 32(4): 378–85.

Watson, A C, Morabito M S, Draine, J and Ottati, V (2008) Improving Police Response to Persons with Mental Illness: A Multi-level Conceptualization of CIT. *International Journal of Law and Psychiatry*, 31: 359–68.

Wax, R (1986) *Doing Fieldwork: Warnings and Advice*. Chicago: University of Chicago Press.

Westley, W (1971) *Violence and the Police: A Sociological Study of Law, Custom and Morality*. Boston, MA: MIT Press.

White, C (2002) Re-assessing the Social Worker's Role as an Appropriate Adult. *Journal of Social Welfare and Family Law*, 24(1): 55–65.

Whitman, J (2003) *Harsh Justice: Criminal Punishment and the Widening Divide Between America and Europe*. Oxford: Oxford University Press.

WHO (2001) The World Health Report 2001 – Mental Health: New Understanding, New Hope [online]. Available at: www.who.int/whr/2001/en/ (accessed 15 December 2015).

WHO (2007) Trenčín Statement on Prisons and Mental Health [online]. Available at: www.euro.who.int/__data/assets/pdf_file/0006/99006/E91402.pdf (accessed 15 December 2015).

WHO (2013) Tuberculosis in Prisons/WHO Global TB Report 2013 [online]. Available at: www.who.int/tb/challenges/prisons/en/ (accessed 15 December 2015).

Wilkinson, R (2000) *Mind the Gap: Hierarchies, Health and Human Evolution*. London: Weidenfeld and Nicholson.

Williams, J (27 October 2010) Are Community Treatment Orders Being Over-used? *The Guardian*.

Wilson, C, Nairn, R, Coverdale, J and Panapa, A (1999) Mental Illness Depictions in Prime-time Drama: Identifying the Discursive Resources. *Australian and New Zealand Journal of Psychiatry*, 33(2): 232–9.

Wilson, J Q (1963) Police and Their Problems: A Theory. *Public Policy*, 12: 189–216.

Wilson, W J (1997) *When Work Disappears: The World of the New Urban Poor*. New York: Vintage.

Wilson, W J (2012) *The Truly Disadvantaged: The Inner City, the Underclass and Public Policy* (2nd edition). Chicago: University of Chicago Press.

Wing, J (1962) Institutionalism in Mental Hospitals. *British Journal of Social and Clinical Psychology*, 1(1): 38–51.

Wing, J (1978) *Reasoning About Madness*. Oxford: Oxford University Press.

Wolch, J and Philo, C (2000) From Distributions of Deviance to Definitions of Difference: Past and Future Mental Health Geographies. *Health and Place*, 6(3): 137–57.

Wolff, N (1998) Interactions Between Mental Health and Law Enforcement Systems: Problems and Prospects for Cooperation. *Journal of Health Politics, Policy and Law*, 23(1): 133–74.

Wolff, N (2005) Community Reintegration of Prisoners with Mental Illness: A Social Investment Perspective. *International Journal of Law and Psychiatry*, 28(1): 43–58.

Wood, J, Swanson, J, Burris, J D and Gilbert, A (2011) *Police Interventions with Persons Affected by Mental Illnesses: A Critical Review of Global Thinking*. New York: Rutgers University Center for Behavioral Health Services and Criminal Justice Research.

Woolf, Lord Justice (1991) *Prison Disturbances April 1990: Report of an Inquiry, February 1991 CM 1456*. London: HMSO.

Yar, M and Penna, S (2004) Between Positivism and Post-modernity? Critical Reflections on Jock Young's The Exclusive Society. *British Journal of Criminology*, 44(4): 533–49.

Yin, R K (1984) *Case Study Research: Design and Methods*. Beverly Hills, CA: Sage Publications.

Young, J (1991) Left Realism and the Priorities of Crime Control, in Stenson, K and Cowell, D (eds), *The Politics of Crime Control*. London: Sage Publications.

Young, J (1999) *The Exclusive Society: Social Exclusion, Crime and Difference in Late Modernity*. London: Sage Publications.

Young, J (2004) Crime and the Dialectics of Inclusion/Exclusion: Some Comments on Yar and Penna. *British Journal of Criminology*, 44(4): 550–6.

Index